THE BIBLE:
NOW I GET IT!

THE BIBLE:
NOW I GET IT!
A Form-Criticism Handbook

GERHARD LOHFINK
Translated by DANIEL COOGAN

Illustrations by Bill Woodman

DOUBLEDAY & COMPANY, INC.
GARDEN CITY, NEW YORK

TRANSLATOR'S NOTE

I am grateful to my son, Professor Michael Coogan of the Harvard Divinity School, for his careful and productive reading of this translation.

D.C.

This book was originally published in German under the title JETZT VERSTEHE ICH DIE BIBEL: EIN SACHBUCH ZUR FORMKRITIK (© 1976 by KBW Verlag, Stuttgart)

Excerpts from *The Jerusalem Bible*, copyright © 1966 by Darton, Longman & Todd, Ltd., and Doubleday & Company, Inc. Used by permission of the publisher.

Library of Congress Cataloging in Publication Data

Lohfink, Gerhard, 1934–
    The Bible—now I get it!
    Translation of Jetzt verstehe ich die Bibel.
    Includes bibliographical references.
    1. Bible—Criticism, Form. I. Title.
BS521.5.L6313   220.6'7
ISBN: 0-385-13432-0
Library of Congress Catalog Card Number 78–1209

For Max Walter

Contents

Introduction

A child says to his mother, "Heaven's up above, isn't it?"—and points upward. "You mean up above, where the clouds and airplanes are?" his mother responds. "No, I mean *really* above," the boy replies, "where God is." Then his mother says, "The heaven where God is isn't only up above. God is everywhere. So heaven is everywhere—in us and around us. The only thing is, we can't see it yet, because first God has to give us different eyes and different feelings."

That's about how a conversation between a little boy and his mother might run these days. Parents who are believers have long known that you can't get to heaven in an airplane. In general they are able to make their children aware of the impossibility of visualizing the heaven of Christian faith.

This fact should not be regarded as something obvious. It wasn't always that way. The detachment of our concepts of life after death from the cosmological concepts of earlier times, which were also the cosmological concepts of the Bible, took place under the greatest difficulties. At some points the process is not altogether complete but still under way. Yet one thing has been achieved: No even moderately normal Christian of today would ever dream of heaven as a place above the clouds or somewhere beyond the Milky Way.

Is the concept "heaven" on that account a closed matter for the modern Christian? Not at all! The concept is just not as much a matter of prime concern as it often used to be. We use the word "heaven" less frequently and with some hesitation, but we do believe in the reality which—beyond all images—was meant by the old idea of heaven. Just as we used to do, we pray "Glory to God in the highest," but we know that we must not understand the concept "high" as having any spatial relevance; at the same time we know that it has meaning. We stay with the image, though we are capable of examining the image more accurately and closely than could Christians of other centuries.

But let us return once more to the mother of whom we spoke at the outset. What will she do when some day her child wants her to tell the story of how the angel Gabriel came to Mary? And what will she answer when, in response to this tale, her child asks her all sorts of questions: Where did the angel come from? How did he get into the house? What did he look like? And, finally, why don't angels come around anymore? Will the same mother, who could handle "heaven" so well, be able to give the right answers then? Is she herself perfectly clear about the nature of the story of the Annunciation in Luke? Does she know that this is a biblical representational form, which one must not confuse with factual account? Can she tell the difference between the outer representational form and the inner meaning in this instance as well?

Probably not. Most parents can't. With regard to narratives such as that of the Annunciation, they have become very uncertain. Even for themselves they have no fixed position. The reason is clear: At this point, for most believers, the process of rethinking belief has begun only in the last two decades. It was not too long ago that narratives of this kind were treated in catechetical instruction as if they were factual reports. All this cannot be quickly brushed aside. Nevertheless, the time will come when parents will know how to differentiate in biblical narratives between the external representational form and the theological statement—just as naturally as they have long distinguished between the "heavens" of the astronauts and the "heaven" of God.

To be sure, this presupposes a certain knowledge of biblical forms of representation, and at least an approximate notion of what is understood in biblical studies today by the term *form criticism*. And here this book may be of some help. It aims to demonstrate that form criticism is not an arcane science for a few highly specialized exegetes; further, that it is not a luxury but a clear necessity. What does the term "form criticism" mean? Let us not begin with an abstract definition, but let us ask first what "form" actually connotes in this context. Let us proceed in our inquiry from the most familiar everyday experiences. Some wonderful surprises are in store for us.

I

FIXED FORMS
IN DAILY LIFE
AND IN LITERATURE

—1—

Letter to Aunt Fanny

Let us assume that someone is writing a letter, and that the letter begins like this:

New York, August 11, 19—

Dear Aunt Fanny,

I haven't written you for a long time. Something always gets in the way. But today the children are gone, so I'll write you, at long last. I am fine, and I hope you are too. The weather has been terrible the last few days. I suppose you had the same in Philadelphia . . .

Have you ever written or received a letter like this?

Well, let's leave this exciting letter to Aunt Fanny. It's just supposed to remind us that when we begin a letter we usually employ fixed forms. A very large number of letters written in America every day begin just the same way as this letter to Aunt Fanny.

Such letter-beginnings can be reduced to the following pattern:

1) an indication of the place where the letter was written,
2) an indication of the date,
3) the name of the recipient (usually with "Dear"),
4) an apology for long neglect,
5) a statement of the writer's good health and an expression of hope that the recipient is in like condition.

Here we have an example of a fixed and often used *form*. The objection could of course be raised that this is all obvious. How else should one begin a letter? Is this "fixed form" not inherent in the very nature of letters? The answer is, not at all! A letter can begin in quite a different way.

When Marcus Tullius Cicero (106–43 B.C.) wrote a letter to his brother Quintus, his letters began like this: "Marcus Quinto fratri salutem" —"Marcus to his brother Quintus, greeting!" In this same short, spare way almost all letters of classical antiquity begin. One could even say simply, "Gaius to Titus." And then the writer turned his attention at once to what is actually on his mind. The naming of the recipient in the direct address form ("Dear Aunt Fanny"), characteristic and almost indispensable in our letters of today, is completely absent in letters from classical times. Furthermore, there is normally no indication of place in the letter from ancient times. Even the date is frequently missing; and if it is there, it is not at the beginning but at the very end of the letter. But what differentiates the form of the classical letter even more sharply from the form usual to us today is the absence of a signature. The short greeting "Vale"—"Fare well!"—was the customary ending of a private Roman letter. No signature was needed, for this, so to speak, was implicit in the heading: "Marcus greets his brother Quintus." So, in classical times we encounter a letter formula quite sharply different from our own.

To be sure, not all of our letters follow the formula of the one to Aunt Fanny. Let's think about official communications or business letters. In contrast to the modern private letter, the recipient's address comes at the beginning. Then come mysterious phrases such as "your invoice number . . . ," "your statement of . . . ," "our invoice number . . . ," "our statement of . . . ," "with reference to. . . ."

These examples make clear that there is a whole series of fixed forms for the beginnings of letters. Almost every letter, consciously or not, relies on one of the customary conventional forms. Anyone familiar with these forms will be able to say at once not only in what century a particular letter was written but also whether the letter in question is a private letter, a business letter, or a letter of some other kind. He will be able to do this *not* from the contents of the letter, let us note, but from its form alone.

SPARKLE & BANG

FIREWORKS MANUFACTURERS

Hissington, Missouri

To: Paul Plupp Co.

    Sissboomton, S. Dak. 57139

Your Invoice No. P/Q
Our Invoice No. Z/Z
Your Statement of: Nov. 11
Our Statement of: Dec. 2

Re: Special Howlers; out-of-stock report

Dear M r. Plupp,

  We are happy to inform you that our SPECIAL HOWLERS

are now back in stock and that your order will be

filled within two weeks. Thank you.

A/A

Shipping Department

Were someone to review all the various forms of letter-beginnings ever used and were he to differentiate among them as to time, function, and social background, he could write a *form history* of letter-beginnings. Such a work would show very clearly in what a formulaic way—from classical antiquity until today—letter-beginnings have been constructed.

2

A Baking Recipe of Cato the Elder

Let us go a step further. Fixed forms exist not only in letter-writing but in a multitude of other situations. Marcus Porcius Cato (234–149 B.C.) recorded in his book *On Farming*—the oldest completely preserved prose work of Latin literature—a whole set of old cooking and baking recipes. A cursory glance suffices to show that they are exactly similar in form to modern recipes. For example, a recipe for cheesecake reads like this:

> Grind two pounds of cheese thoroughly in a mortar. After grinding well, add one pound of winter wheat flour, or, for gourmet palates, one-half pound of the finest wheat flour, and stir it thoroughly with the cheese. Add one egg and stir well. Shape a cake from the mixture, wrap it in leaves, and bake it lightly in a warm stove under an earthenware dish.
>
> [DE AGRI CULTURA 75]

Taking into account that the modern housewife no longer grinds cheese in a mortar, and uses aluminum foil rather than leaves to wrap things in, it is hardly noticeable that Cato's recipe is over two thousand years old. What is lacking is only the familiar "Take" which is a part of the generic style of cooking recipes in our day. Here then we have before us a linguistic form that has not changed but has been preserved over a long period of time.

What is essential for the form of the cooking recipe is a detailed indication of the ingredients and an exact description of the process of preparation in the correct order. This description consists of a series of relatively short sentences, each of which contains a specific requirement. Cooking recipes in their linguistic structure are closely related to the form of *directions*

The modern kitchen and the ancient Roman kitchen are differently furnished, and cooking and baking recipes have also undergone substantial change. The linguistic *form* of the recipe, however, has remained almost completely unaltered over the centuries.

for use. Directions for use also consist of a framework of short instructions, which generally must be listed in a given sequence: ("First. . . . Next. . . . Finally. . . .") Cooking recipes and directions for use are concise, closely joined instructions that tacitly presuppose that the product in question is good, tested, reliable.

3

Death Notices

There are many other examples of linguistic forms, preserved with astonishing uniformity. We open the obituary page of almost any newspaper and read:

> McTavish, Celia Rose, 85, widow of Nigel Thomas McTavish, on July 29, 197–, in Huntsville, Maryland. Survivors are daughter, Mrs. George W. Johnson, granddaughter Alice Parry Smith and great-granddaughter Louise Jean Smith. Memorial service at the Methodist Church, Huntsville, Tuesday, August 2, 197–, at 2:00 p.m. Interment Calvary Cemetery, Huntsville. In lieu of flowers contributions may be made to the Methodist Memorial Fund, Huntsville.

So here too is a fixed, stereotypic form, which is well established down to the smallest details, and which for centuries has remained almost unchanged.

Three hundred years ago an obituary notice might have read like this:

> In the year 1651, on Sunday, April 27,
> between midnight and one o'clock
> the late virtuous Maria Bülgin
> of the White Mill, née Walfmann,
> fell asleep gently and happily
> in her Redeemer Jesus Christ.
> She was 22 years, 2 months, 2 days old.
> God have mercy on her soul.
> Amen.

This is the text of an epitaph found on the left side wall of the church of Detwang, a village near the German town of Rothenburg-ob-der-Tauber. I copied it many years ago on a trip through the Tauber valley because the language of the inscription and all the deep emotional piety implied in this language profoundly touched me. A long time later, as I was going over my notes, I came upon this inscription again and was suddenly struck by its *formal* similarity to our modern obituary notices. The language, of course, is different. Yet the text, in its basic structure, corresponds with considerable exactness to the newspaper text just quoted. A form-critical analysis shows this very readily. The two texts have in common:

1) the name of the deceased,
2) a short description of the deceased,
3) the age of the deceased,
4) the date of death.

Because of this congruence, form criticism would classify the Detwang text, even though it is an inscription, as a death notice. Today it is our custom to publish death notices in the newspaper or to circulate them in the form of letters. But in the seventeenth century a death notice obviously could be published also in the form of an inscription. We see very clearly by this example that a definite form can be preserved, while the nature of its publication is radically changed.

Observations of this kind can become very important for form-critical investigations. Thus, for example, the nature of the publication of "narrative" has completely changed. We *read* narratives today in the newspaper or in books. But formerly narratives were really narrated—told by word of mouth. They were not read but listened to, as told by someone who was a master of the technique of telling. When we come upon narratives in the Bible, we see that they are often genuine *tales*, planned and formed in the first instance for oral delivery. They were frequently committed to writing at a relatively late point in time.

—— 4 ————————————————

The Solemn Beginning of a Sermon

Fixed forms then are not found only in written statements. Speech too is frequently couched in fixed and preordained forms. Just a few decades ago a preacher might have begun his Pentecost sermon like this:

"Suddenly there came a sound from heaven as of a mighty wind coming: and it filled the whole house in which they were sitting." Words taken from the Acts of the Apostles, chapter two, verse two.

Dearly beloved in the Lord, we assemble today for the Feast of Pentecost. . . .

This form for the beginning of a sermon was at one time very much in favor. It consists of

    1) a text (usually from the bible),
    2) the citation for the text,
    3) a solemn salutation of the congregation,
       with mention of the reason for the sermon.

When a sermon began in this form, people generally knew that it would last at least a half hour! The solemn beginning and the length of the sermon were related. Today sermons are shorter, often use no text, and are prefaced in other ways.

So then sermon beginnings too have fixed forms, and here, too, without any problem, a form history of sermon beginnings—that is, a history of the forms of all sermon beginnings that have ever been in use—could be written. It would certainly be very interesting. It would show what social and theological rank was attributed in each era to the listening congregation. Such a form history of sermon beginnings would reveal, for example, that in the fourth century the congregation could be addressed as "your holiness" (sanctitas vestra)—a form of address which was later granted not to the whole congregation but to the pope alone.

Fixed forms of oral discourse are found in divine worship not only at the beginning of the sermon but in many other places. Without exaggeration we can say that every liturgy presents a firm framework of defined forms of oral discourse. The reason is clear: Every act of human speech that is repeated at regular intervals and that always has the same hearers and the same content is naturally inclined to formalization. One good illustration of this is the classic Roman Catholic collect. Originally the collect was a prayer freely formulated for each occasion by whoever presided at the liturgy, but soon fixed laws of structure became established, which ultimately led to the classic form. The form is wonderfully clear and simple. No translation can match the flow of its utterance. One of the finest examples is the former collect for the Third Sunday after Pentecost:

Oremus.
Protector in te sperantium, Deus, sine quo nihil est validum, nihil
   sanctum: multiplica super nos misericordiam tuam, ut et rectore, te
   duce,

sic transeamus per bona temporalia,
ut non amittamus aeterna—per dominum nostrum Jesum Christum
   filium tuum, qui tecum vivit et regnat in unitate Spiritus Sancti,
per omnia saecula saeculorum.
Amen.

Let us pray.
O God, Protector of those who hope in Thee,
without Whom nothing is healthy, nothing holy,
increase Thy mercy upon us;
that under Thy direction and guidance
we may so pass through the good things of this life
that we lose not those which are eternal: through Jesus Christ Thy
   Son, our Lord, Who liveth and reigneth with Thee in the unity of
   the Holy Spirit
forever and ever.
Amen.

The structure of this collect is easy to grasp. The prayer is divided into six parts:

> 1) an invitation to prayer,
> 2) an invocation of God,
> 3) an extension of the invocation,
> 4) a petition,
> 5) a solemn closing formula,
> 6) a ratification of the prayer by the congregation.

Even the structure permits us to see clearly the nature of this prayer. By the invitation at the beginning (Oremus) and the ratification at the end (Amen) the text is clearly defined as a prayer of the community. The celebrant speaks it as a representative of the community. The clause "without Whom nothing is healthy, nothing holy" is simply an extension of the invocation. The actual main part of the prayer is contained in the petitions, and our collect must be defined as a prayer of petition.

The formal structure here described is present in the majority of Roman collects. Form-critically, therefore, this type of collect must be defined as a short prayer of petition with an extended invocation and a solemn formulaic close. The prayer is spoken by the leader of the assembly in the name of the community.

The form of the opening of a sermon has changed over time as much as the shape of the pulpit itself. One who was familiar with the history of Christian preaching could write a history of sermon openings and their relationship to other circumstances in Christian life.

— 5 —————————

Conversations at the End of the Working Day

Fixed forms of oral discourse, however, do not exist only in the realm of the liturgy. Our speech can sound as if constructed according to a pattern in the midst of everyday life—often without our noticing it. A style of speech formalized in this way easily comes into being when we get into specific, frequently recurring situations of conversation. The German writer Kurt Tucholsky, who was a great observer of such things, has described a great number of such typical situations, in which language is used in accordance with fixed forms: telephone conversations, dialogues between business people, a family quarrel. Best of all, however, is his sketch of a conversation between a couple who are getting rid of the vexations of a day at the office by talking when they meet in the evening:

> He goes to meet her at work or vice versa. The couple take a little walk to limber up; the evening air is refreshing after the long hours at work. They tell each other about their day. And what was it like? Aggravation. There is a saying that you can button your lip, but it isn't quite true. It comes unbuttoned. At the time you can't even talk back to the boss or your fellow worker or the elevator operator. But the button comes off at 5 P.M.
>
> He tells her how it was at work today. First the report. Have you ever observed the way such battles are reported? The reporter comes off as a model of tranquillity and patience, the opponent is a howling savage. It goes about like this: "I said, 'Mr. Winkler,' I said—'that new filing system won't work!'" (This is said in the quietest tone in the world, mild, detached, wise.) "He said, 'I beg your pardon!' he said—'I designed this system personally!'" (This is said quickly, violently, angrily.) Now the cool head again: "I said, very quietly, I said, 'Mr. Winkler,' I said, 'we can't file letters like that, or else the C mail will get mixed up with the D mail!'"

The description of the dispute at work continues; it reaches its climax and breaks off with the question "Can you beat that?" "Girlfriend" finds it scandalous, of course, and for boyfriend that is a great comfort. Then the roles are exchanged. Now she tells about the atrocious behavior of the girls in her office. And he finds *this* scandalous. So each one gets comfort, and psychic equilibrium is restored. And this was exactly the purpose of the whole conversation. The entire form of the representation ("'Mr. Winkler,' I said—'that new filing system won't work'") was unconscious, yet designed with the greatest singleness of purpose to justify the narrator's behavior and to obtain the approval and agreement of his/her partner. All the description was aimed at the question "Can you beat that?" This goal determined the form of the representation. A description which aimed at objective criticism by the partner would have appeared quite different, not only in content but especially in form.[1]

Conversations like Tucholsky's sketch take place of course not only between lovers, and not only after work. Whenever we report an event in which we ourselves are involved, and want to assure ourselves of the approving agreement of our partner, our language can assume the same form.

— 6 —

Greetings in the Arabian Desert

In everyday life a multitude of other typical conversational forms exist. These are used especially when certain situations are regularly repeated. Examples: a doctor questioning his patient, an oral examination, a sales pitch, a social introduction, advice from a confessor, greetings, farewells, debate, official consultation, exchange of experiences, an interview, a newscast.

If you undertook an investigation of oral communications of this kind, with careful regard to beginning, conclusion, entire structure, and regularly recurring concepts and formulas, you would probably be quite astonished to see how much of our daily life is regulated by fixed forms of speech.

Now it is important to know that in the East, to which great portions of the Bible belong socially and culturally, the language and behavior of the people are much more strongly ritualized even than with us. For example, when Easterners greet one another, a ceremony occurs which is even more formal than the greetings to which we are accustomed. W. Thesiger, who traveled in Southern Arabia from 1945 to 1950, reports an encounter in the desert:

> When they were a few yards away Mahsin, whom I identified by his lame leg, called out "Salam Alaikum," and we answered together "Alaikum es Salam." Then one behind the other they passed along our line, greeting each of us with the triple nose-kiss, nose touching nose on the right side, left side, and again on the right. They then formed up facing us. Tamtaim said to me, "Ask their news"; but I answered, "No, you do it. You are the oldest." Tamtaim called out, "Your news?" Mahsin answered, "The news is good." Again Tamtaim asked, "Is anyone dead? Is anyone gone?" Back came the immediate answer, "No!—don't say such a thing." Question and answer were as invariable as the responses in the Litany. No matter what had really happened, they never changed. They might have fought with raiders; half their party might have been killed and be lying still unburied; their camels might have been looted; any affliction might have befallen them—starvation, drought, or sickness, and still at this first formal questioning they would answer, "The news is good."[2]

A greeting ritual of this kind may seem at first glance to be strange and meaningless. But if one looks closer, one sees very soon that there are ritual greetings of this kind, in modified form, here in our own culture. Let us take as an example the following exchange, of a type with which we are all familiar.

> A. Morning!
> B. Morning!
> A. How are you?
> B. Fine, thanks!
> A. Terrible weather, isn't it?
> B. It sure is.

Most of the elements of this greeting have lost their original linguistic significance. At the very least the question "How are you?" and the answer "Fine, thanks!" have a ritual character. The person who asks the question is generally not interested in the health of the other person. And the one who answers "Fine, thanks!" may be very sick at the moment of response. But the rite requires nonetheless that he answer "Fine, thanks!" Correctly so, for the question "How are you?" in such a greeting generally does not aim at ascertaining genuine information but at establishing a community of interest. Linguistics (the science dealing with the formal laws of utterance) would express it this way: Question and answer do not here aim at getting

In typical, recurring conversation situations, conversation runs in fixed, predetermined forms.

"WHERE DOES IT HURT?"

information but at opening communication. Once this has happened, by means of the more or less ritual exchange of the greeting, it is quite possible for a conversation to result in which there is exhaustive and informative discussion about health,˙ financial situation, anxiety about the children's problems, and so on. The difference from the greeting in the desert, then, is not so great after all.

Thus in greetings we have a human speech utterance which can have a fixed form, and this form in turn has quite a fixed function and a fixed actual setting. Once we are aware of this and keep our eyes open, we can find everywhere in daily life such fixed forms, which are common to everyone, which are always applied on the same occasion ("actual setting" or *Sitz im Leben*), and which one takes over for oneself consciously or unconsciously again and again because it would be too much trouble to work out new forms. It is important to watch these forms with great care, to examine what particular function they serve.

— **7** —————————————————

From the Poem to the Novel

In what has been said so far we have been concerned with definite, fixed, permanent forms of everyday life. But there are also fixed forms in literature. When a writer sets down on paper things that move him and that he would like to communicate to others, he considers carefully what form will be most suitable to his purpose.

For a scientist, for example, it makes a great difference whether he is writing an essay for a scientific periodical, an article in a specialized encyclopedia, or an article for the daily popular science column in the newspaper. In an article for an encyclopedia he can list scientific data without much introduction or transition; a discussion of individual results of investigations is not necessary. By contrast, the essay for a specialized periodical requires an intensive exposition of the investigative results of other scientists. In this respect footnotes can be especially helpful: They relieve the actual text of numerical data, citations, and other details. In a newspaper article, on the other hand, there are neither notes nor a mere listing of data. Here one

We read a detective novel with one set of expectations and a biography with another, for the two lay hold of reality in different ways.

must have a careful introduction and carefully considered transitions between the facts reported, for the newspaper article is written for the nonspecialist.

We are more clearly aware of the various literary forms in so-called belles-lettres. The materials for poems, epics, dramas, short stories, novellas, and novels are treated in completely different fashion. Each of these forms or genres has its own laws; not every one is suitable for the same material. Or, in other words, a writer is not permitted to choose any form at will, nor can one change literary forms as one changes one's clothes. Subject matter relating to crime can be represented very well in the form of a novel (Dostoyevsky provides the best example in *The Brothers Karamazov*) but not usually in the form of a poem. And the experience of a full, rich moment can be expressed in the form of a poem—but certainly not in the form of a novel. Thus every literary form reveals, in its own way, the truth; therefore, we approach every literary form with different expectations.

One expects from a classical novel a manifold variety of figures; one expects various mises-en-scène, spaciousness, societal interrelations; one expects a piece of a "world" as rich, many-layered, and complex as the very world we live in. But naturally one does not expect that the characters in the novel were ever alive, or, if it is a "historical" novel, that they said and did everything said and done by the author's characters.

A reader of the great book by Boswell about Johnson likewise will expect a multitude of figures, the description of various scenes of action, the representation of developments and societal interrelations; he will expect a "piece of the world"—that is, a description of the world to which Johnson belonged. But of course he expects that all the figures who appear in this book really were alive at one time and that in principle the only events recounted are those which really took place. He expects neither the writer's impressions nor his confessions but, on the contrary, objective historical analyses and well-balanced judgments.

A reader of an autobiography also expects a multitude of figures; he expects various scenes of action, developments, societal interrelations. But the piece of "world" which he hopes to discover is the world of the author or the world from the author's point of view. In this case too the reader expects the facts communicated to him to be correct. Nevertheless he understands inexactitudes, errors, or lapses of memory. What interests him is above all the individual point of view of the author, his way of experiencing the world, his personal impressions and memories. In this case the reader expects confessional statements, partiality, and subjectivity.

One could continue in this vein for a long time. We approach a poem with different expectations than we do a short story; we approach a fairy tale with different expectations than we do a drama. Again, our expectations are different in regard to a collection of proverbs, a heroic saga, a novella, or a radio play. All these linguistic forms deal with and reveal truth, but each in a different way.

It is surely obvious how important it is for the correct understanding of a text to know as exactly as possible in what literary form it speaks to us. For only then does one know how it reveals the truth. This is true of course for the Bible as well as for any kind of literature.

The weather map is a relatively new linguistic form. (© 1978 *by the New York Times Company. Reprinted by permission.*)

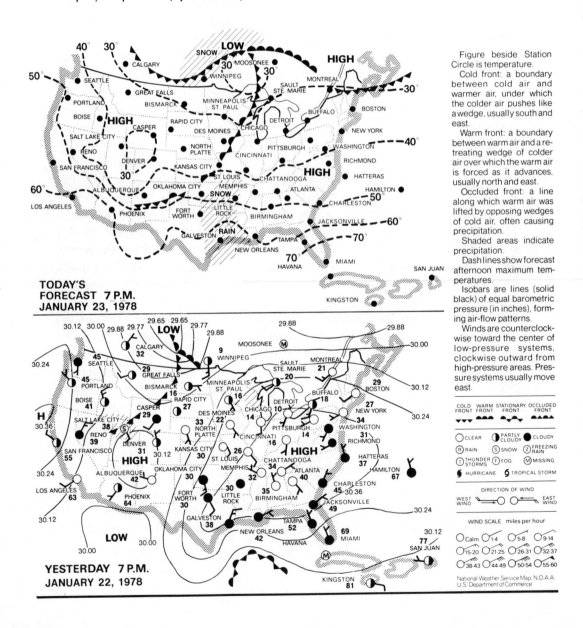

TODAY'S FORECAST 7 P.M. JANUARY 23, 1978

YESTERDAY 7 P.M. JANUARY 22, 1978

Figure beside Station Circle is temperature.

Cold front: a boundary between cold air and warmer air, under which the colder air pushes like a wedge, usually south and east.

Warm front: a boundary between warm air and a retreating wedge of colder air over which the warm air is forced as it advances, usually north and east.

Occluded front: a line along which warm air was lifted by opposing wedges of cold air, often causing precipitation.

Shaded areas indicate precipitation.

Dash lines show forecast afternoon maximum temperatures.

Isobars are lines (solid black) of equal barometric pressure (in inches), forming air-flow patterns.

Winds are counterclockwise toward the center of low-pressure systems, clockwise outward from high-pressure areas. Pressure systems usually move east.

National Weather Service Map. N.O.A.A. U.S. Department of Commerce

── II ──

WHAT IS FORM CRITICISM?

After these extensive considerations we do not now need to look very long for a definition of form criticism. *Form criticism concerns itself with fixed forms of the kind described—in everyday life or in literature, in the oral and written statements of human beings; it means, simply, to discover these forms, to describe them, to determine their linguistic intent, and to determine their actual setting* (Sitz im Leben).

In the following pages we will express a few thoughts about these four steps of form criticism.

— 1 —

The Discovery of Fixed Forms

In 1930 André Jolles wrote his famous book *Einfache Formen* (*Simple Forms*).[3] In this work he investigated speech forms such as legend, saga, riddle, saying, fairy tale, and joke. He attempted to work out the characteristic, special features of each of these forms. A book like Jolles's shows that for form criticism the age of discovery began after World War I. It has not ended even today, for sound reasons.

First, the number of fixed, determinate forms is not constant but continually increasing. Technical and cultural developments always create new situations for human beings, and every new situation in which man is involved necessarily produces new forms of speaking. Thus, for example, weather reports have become crystallized in the last few decades as a determinate form, with a fixed structure and a constant style (current conditions . . . forecast . . . extended forecast). This could only come about when two factors were present: (1) scientific research of the weather (modern meteorology) and (2) daily transmission of up-to-date information to a large group of receivers (modern communications media). When both factors were present, the weather report was born as a new linguistic form.

In literature new forms and genres continually arise. A literary form like the following is simply not found in the literature of past centuries. Here is a text by Reinhard Lettau, published in 1963.

Scene

A gentleman comes in.
"It's me," he says.
"Try again!" we cry.
He comes in again.
"Here I am," he says.
"It's not much better," we cry.
He enters the room again.
"I'm the one," he says.

"A poor start," we cry.

He comes in once more.

"Hello!" he calls. He waves.

"Please don't!" we say.

He tries again.

"Here I am again!" he calls.

"Almost!" we exclaim.

He comes in again.

"The fellow you've been waiting for so long," he says.

"Do it again!" we cry, but alas, now we have hesitated too long, now he stays outside, doesn't want to come in anymore, has disappeared, we don't see him anymore, even when we open the front door and give a quick look down the street in both directions.[4]

What linguistic form does this represent? A little drama? A short story? A similitude? None of these designations of genre fits our text. The action consists of a single scene, which is extremely jejune. The actors are neither introduced nor described. The identity of "we" is undisclosed. Nor is it said who "the gentleman" is, whence he comes, or where he goes. The atmosphere of narrative, otherwise usual in short stories, which presupposes a faithful reproduction of reality, is transparent. The narrative takes place as if reality were being described in the form of a similitude, but the text is not a similitude. The last sentence, upon which everything else converges, resembles events in a dream, but our text is not presented as a dream.

Texts of this kind appear in German literature for the first time in the works of Franz Kafka (1883–1924); there are many examples of them. It is clear that a new literary form has come into being, specially adapted to expressing the complex experiences of the twentieth century. For the form of these texts is open on all sides; it is not obvious; it is fragmented—just like the experiences of modern writers. Literary scholarship has as yet no correct name for such texts; at present we simply call them "short prose." So here we have a field in which future form criticism has many discoveries still to make.

But it is not only the discovery of nascent linguistic structures which constantly broadens our knowledge of fixed forms and genres. The era of discovery for linguistic utterances of the past is by no means over. Thus, for example, in the last few decades many new forms have been discovered whose existence was previously unsuspected. How do such discoveries take place?

We know from his letters that Paul had a vision of Christ outside Damascus. Early Christian tradition portrays this event with formal elements from the Old Testament, shaping the vision on the model of the Old Testament "apparition dialogue." (*Woodcut by Hans Baldung; reproduction courtesy of the New York Public Library Picture Collection.*)

Let us assume that a biblical scholar is investigating the text of Acts 9:3–6, in which Paul's vocation is described. The text reads:

> Suddenly, while he was traveling to Damascus and just before he reached the city, there came a light from heaven all round him. He fell to the ground, and then he heard a voice saying, "Saul, Saul, why are you persecuting me?" "Who are you, Lord?" he asked, and the voice answered, "I am Jesus, and you are persecuting me. Get up now and go into the city, and you will be told what you have to do."

We notice in this text that the heavenly voice calls Paul twice running by his Hebrew name. For a form-critical investigation such stylistic phenomena often furnish very valuable hints. So it is appropriate to compare other biblical texts in which the doubling of the name occurs, with, of course, an effort at complete documentation. For this the exegete must, to be sure, read through the entire Bible. For no reference book exists in which stylistic phenomena such as name doubling are compiled. At this time no computer can as yet solve this problem, but the task of reading through the Bible is rewarding, for it turns out that the repeated use of a name is by no means a rarity. What is more, in some of the biblical texts in which a name is used twice we have, as in Acts 9:3–6, accounts of apparitions.

Our attention must now be devoted to these accounts of apparitions with name repetition. In the course of his investigation, the researcher writes them down alongside each other and compares them closely. In this way it becomes clear that some of these texts are formally constructed in a way quite similar to Acts 9:3–6. The most interesting parallel is Genesis 46:1–3. This text reads:

> Israel [=Jacob] left with his possessions and reached Beersheba. There he offered sacrifices to the God of his father Isaac. God spoke to Israel in a vision at night, He said. "Jacob, Jacob." He replied, "I am here." He continued, "I am God, the God of your father. Do not be afraid of going down to Egypt, for I will make you a great nation there."

The Old Testament and the New Testament texts are constructed according to the following pattern:

1) description of the situation,
2) introduction of speech,
3) double summons by the appearing being,
4) introduction of speech,
5) response of the person confronted by the apparition,
6) introduction of speech,
7) self-revelation of apparition,
8) charge to person confronted.

Such similarity of formal structure in several apparitional texts, from widely separated passages of the Bible, cannot be accidental. Further investigation reveals that in other Jewish writings that are not part of the Bible apparitions can be narrated according to the same formal pattern. It is no longer possible to doubt: In the Old Testament and in other Jewish literature there was manifestly a set pattern that could be used to tell an impressive story of a dialogue between a heavenly apparition and a human being;[5] this pattern occurs in the New Testament as well, namely in Acts. Conclusion: A new formal pattern has been discovered, exact knowledge of which is very important for the interpretation and critique of the apparition texts concerned.

Of course the discovery of a fixed linguistic form can take a very different course. This practical example was meant to show that despite fifty years of biblical form criticism the age of discoveries is by no means past.

—— 2 ——

The Description of Fixed Forms

Once a linguistic form has been discovered, it should next be described as minutely as possible. That is often not as easy as it appears at first glance. For not every form is constructed as stereotypically and schematically as the apparition dialogue just described. Thus, for example, jokes are surely a special, self-contained form of human discourse. But what makes a joke a joke? How can what is typical in a joke be linguistically understood and described? Another example: In all modern "Introductions to the Old Testament," *saga* is cited as a special genre of biblical narrative.[6] And quite rightly! But what constitutes the form of biblical sagas? What is the difference between sagas and stories of some other kind? How can the differences be described formally—that is, from the point of view of linguistic structure?

It is naturally simplest when the form to be described is permeated with characteristic words and unchanging formulas. Thus most fairy tales begin with "Once upon a time . . . ," and it has become usual to close them with a formula such as ". . . and they lived happily ever after."

If we encounter somewhere phrases such as "very respectfully yours," "sincerely," "best regards," "gratefully," or "fondly," it is clear that we have

" DID YOU HEAR THE
ONE ABOUT THE
GUY WHO...

Even the joke is a special and quite consistent form of human speech. The characteristic "punch line" always comes at the end.

a letter before us. If, on the other hand, we meet such expressions as "departed from us," "deceased," "the late lamented," "honored memory," "rest in peace," or "in deep sympathy," we know that we are dealing with a death notice. In such cases we speak of the generic style of a form. In the case of the form of the apparition dialogue, for example, the duplication of address and the self-revelation of the apparition with the words "I am . . ." belong to the generic style.

To describe a fixed linguistic form, more is required than just the working out of the generic style. We must also examine the form concerned to ascertain whether it begins with typical, ever-present form elements. Such form elements became familiar to us in beginnings of letters: indication of the date, salutation. Another example is provided by the Old Testament hymn. From the form-critical point of view it always begins with an introduction which invites the participants to solemn praise of God. In Psalm 33 we have a hymn in which the introduction and the main portion of the hymn are very clearly emphasized.

> Shout for joy to Yahweh, all virtuous men,
> praise comes well from upright hearts;
> give thanks to Yahweh on the lyre,
> play to him on the ten-string harp;
> sing a new song in his honor,
> play with all your skill as you acclaim him!
> For the word of Yahweh is integrity itself,
> all he does is done faithfully. . . .
>
> [PSALM 33:1–4]

The introduction to the hymn is clearly recognizable by the five invitations: "Shout for joy," "give thanks . . . on the lyre," "play . . . on the ten-string harp," "sing," "play with . . . skill." The transition to the main portion of the hymn is marked by the word "For." Introduced by this shift, the reasons are listed for which Yahweh deserves praise and jubilation. An *invitation* to praise, on the other hand, is no longer forthcoming. The introductory portion, then, closes with the words "as you acclaim him!" All Old Testament hymns begin in a similar way. Thus we have in the hymn a linguistic form which reveals itself by its opening words.

It is clear why a linguistic form, especially in the beginning, is apt to follow prescribed form elements. The beginning, after all, must make clear to the hearer or reader what kind of speech utterance is to be used in what follows. Furthermore, the beginning is often the most difficult in both writing and speaking. Therefore we are most likely to adhere to a fixed, generally current pattern in the beginning.

Similar circumstances determine the conclusion of a fixed form. Here too language is likely to follow structures already in existence. Thus the Old Testament hymn in general has not only an introductory passage but also a clearly marked conclusion. The oration of the Roman liturgy closes with a solemn formulaic line. Paul's epistles, without exception, end with a prayer for blessing, in liturgical style. Even narratives end in most cases with a schematic conclusion, which, to be sure, can be variously designed. The miracle stories of the Synoptic Gospels often end in a "choral conclusion," consisting in emphasis on the admiring praise of the spectators. Examples:

> The people were so astonished that they started asking each other what it all meant. "Here is a teaching that is new," they said, "and with authority behind it: he gives orders even to unclean spirits and they obey him."
>
> [MARK 1:27]

And the man got up, picked up his stretcher at once and walked out in front of everyone, so that they were all astounded and praised God, saying, "We have never seen anything like this." [MARK 2:12]

They were filled with awe and said to one another, "Who can this be? Even the winds and the sea obey him." [MARK 4:41]

Their admiration was unbounded. "He has done all things well," they said. "He makes the deaf hear and the dumb speak." [MARK 7:37]

Everyone was filled with awe and praised God, saying, "A great prophet has appeared among us; God has visited his people." [LUKE 7:16]

This form of choral conclusion at the end of miracle stories exists not only in the Gospels but also in pagan miracle stories of that time. Thus we have a fixed, widespread pattern.

The examples cited have surely indicated that in the description of an established form special attention must be paid to both beginning and conclusion. Of course the question as to whether the main portion is constructed according to a fixed pattern must also not be neglected. We have already become acquainted with several forms which manifest a consistent structural pattern, such as the Roman collect and the apparition dialogue.

— 3 —

The Concept of Linguistic Intent

This naturally does not account for everything. To describe an established linguistic form one must not limit oneself simply to investigation of the external structure of the form in question. Much more subtle questions must be asked.

One of these questions, for example, must be, "What kind of speech is present in the form to be described? What purpose or goal does this speaking have? Is it intended for information, narration, didactic purposes, or proclamation? Does it aim at accusation, admonition, or confession?"

Very different forms and genres result from these varying basic aims of speech. It is quite possible that one cannot easily guess the basic intent from the external structure of the text but must first uncover this by a careful linguistic analysis. For this reason it is not enough to describe only the external structural laws of a genre. One simply must ask about the intent. Insight into what a specific speech form actually intends is absolutely decisive for explanation and interpretation. We have already seen that a novel has a different intention from an autobiography. Let us clarify the meaning of linguistic intent for interpretation by a much simpler example, which we have likewise already encountered.

Someone asks another person, "How are you?" and the latter replies, "Fine, thanks!" As we saw, this question and answer serve only very rarely the purpose of collecting information. In general in these forms of dialogue one is not concerned with exchange of information but with the establishment or ratification of common interest (communication). Therefore, if the interlocutor in such a dialogue answers, "Fine, thanks!" (even if he is miserable), he is not lying. He only intended to express with those words: "I'm glad to take up communication with you."

Another example: Someone says to another person, "I love you!" What kind of language is this? If it is just a question of information, it would be quite appropriate for the person addressed just to take note of the information in a practical sense. He might say, "Fine. That's O.K." But suppose the basic linguistic intent is not informational but confessional—of the highest emotional intensity. Then "Fine. That's O.K." would be a terrible answer. For one can only answer such a confession by a refusal or a confession of one's own. Insight into this kind of human speech in this example, therefore, is a matter of totally decisive significance. The same is true of every form of human discourse: What is its purpose, its basic intent? Here description of a specific form or genre is brought to its most important point.

But are not all these mere matters of course? Why so much discussion? Who could ever misunderstand a form of human speech like "I love you"? We can't be too sure. Perhaps many bitter disappointments are caused just by the fact that confessional statements are regarded as and responded to as pieces of information. But one thing in any case is clear. In the history of the Church infinite confusion and inestimable harm have resulted from the fact that inadequate attention was paid to the basic intent of specific genres and forms. Biblical texts intended as proclamations were thought to be reports. New Testament texts whose purpose was to admonish were thought to be laws. And ecclesiastical texts which had a confessional purpose were regarded as informational data. Opposition to a definite form of ecclesiastical dogma and of dogmatic definitions, which is widespread, only came about because the Church made claim with increasing

The context in which a message is received can conceal its intent and so change its effect. To receive a declaration of love as raw information is to deliver an insult, however excusably under some circumstances!

frequency that she was delivering factual information about God by means of creedal statements. But in the Bible creedal statements were never considered to be factual information. They were, in form, clearly confessions, awestruck and grateful confessions of God's saving deeds. It is high time to provide dogma once again with this form of language.

— 4 —

The Actual Setting (*Sitz im Leben*)

In the three previous sections we were concerned with the discovery and description of fixed linguistic forms and with the concept of linguistic intent. Now, to understand correctly what form criticism is, we must also speak of the so-called "actual setting" (*Sitz im Leben*). The expression was first used by the Old Testament scholar Hermann Gunkel (1862–1932), who introduced form criticism as a method in modern biblical scholarship. What does biblical scholarship mean by this strange designation?

We can best start with another example: We have already become acquainted with the Old Testament genre of the hymn. We have seen that the hymn has a fixed structure: It begins with an introduction which invites the people to praise God. Then follows the main portion, in which the praise of God is justified by enumeration of his salutary deeds. At the end comes a short concluding passage, which often expresses a wish or a petition. The exact knowledge of this structure is very important for the interpretation of a hymn. But just as important for the interpretation is the question, Where and on what occasion were such hymns actually sung?

To find an answer to this question, we must examine the Old Testament hymns ourselves, especially their introductions. We then discover: (1) In the overwhelming majority of the hymns a community rather than an individual is invited to praise God. Example, Psalm 149:1: ". . . let the congregation of the faithful sing his praise!" (2) Hymns were apparently not prayed but sung. Example, Psalm 98:1: "Sing Yahweh a new song. . . ." (3) This singing is not unaccompanied but is aided by the sound of musical instruments. Example, Psalm 150:3–4: "Praise him with blasts of the trumpet, praise him with lyre and harp, praise him with drums and dancing, praise him with strings and reeds. . . ." (4) Hymns were sung not just anywhere but in the temple. Example, Psalm 150:1: "Praise God in his temple on earth, praise him in his temple in heaven. . . ." The Old Testament hymns themselves show by their introductions that the hymn is a song, sung on gala occasions in the temple, with musical accompaniment. Thus the hymn has its actual setting in the worship of the temple.

Similarly each form or genre of the Old Testament can be examined on the basis of its setting. This examination shows that many more Old Testament genres originally had to do with the temple or other holy places than one might assume at first glance.

Everyone who prays the 150 psalms of the Psalter regularly has no doubt noticed how uncommonly often individuals are there mentioned who maliciously accuse an innocent person, persecute him, and try to kill him. Why does this theme play such a large role in the psalms? The explanation is simple: In Israel, in exceptionally difficult legal cases which an ordinary judge could not decide, one would have recourse to the central sanctuary and there have a priest give a "divine" judgment. The accused first besought God for his judgment and at the same time solemnly declared his own innocence. But this was done in a psalm—either in one originally composed or in one which the priests had on hand as a formulary. Such a prayer of the accused before the "divine" judgment might run like this:

> Yahweh my God, I take shelter in you;
> from all who hound me, save me, rescue me,
> or, like a lion, he will carry me off
> and tear me to pieces where no one can save me.
> Yahweh my God, if I ever
> soiled my hands with fraud,
> repaid a friend evil for good,
> spared a man who wronged me,
> then let the enemy hound me down and catch me,
> let him stamp my life into the ground,
> and leave my entrails lying in the dust!
> Give judgment for me, Yahweh: as my virtue
>   and my integrity deserve.
> bring the maliciousness of evil men to an end,
>   set the virtuous on his feet. . . .

[PSALM 7:1–5, 8–9]

In this prayer the supplicant has sought refuge in the sanctuary. In an oath he asserts his innocence, with unconditional self-malediction should he be guilty, and begs for a righteous decision from God. In the background of Psalm 7, accordingly, there stands an old juridical procedure which took

Many categories of Old Testament speech had their setting in the temple cult. One example is the hymn that was sung with musical accompaniment during worship in the temple. Here we see a model of the Herodian temple. (*Photo by Joerg Zink, Stuttgart.*)

place in an Israelite sanctuary. The same background is present in many other psalms. Apparently these very prayer formulas of the kind described were especially strongly favored when the psalms were being collected. Thus we must not be surprised when persecutors and those innocently accused are so often mentioned. Much in the psalms cannot be understood unless their original actual setting is grasped. In general it is hard to understand many Old Testament forms and genres unless one knows that their scene was originally in the sanctuary or in the temple.

For the New Testament the Jewish temple of course no longer plays any role. But, as in the Old Testament, many of the forms and genres of the New Testament come from the divine worship of the congregation. The form-critical work of the last decades has isolated a whole set of songs, liturgical formulas, and creedal statements that originated in the primitive Christian liturgy. In epistolary literature of the New Testament and the Johannine Apocalypse a great deal of liturgical tradition has been absorbed by the various writers.

Of course it is an important question whether the four Gospels also contain forms and genres that originally had their setting in community worship. There has been a lot of reflection about this problem. For example, in Matthew, Mark, and Luke there are a number of relatively short, rounded-off, and self-contained stories that have an instructive character and no interest in long descriptions and details. On the contrary, their purpose and climax consists of a single saying of Jesus. Mark 2:18–20 is a good illustration:

> One day when John's disciples and the Pharisees were fasting, some people came and said to him, "Why is it that John's disciples and the disciples of the Pharisees fast, but your disciples do not?" Jesus replied, "Surely the bridegroom's attendants would never think of fasting while the bridegroom is still with them? As long as they have the bridegroom with them, they could not think of fasting. But the time will come for the bridegroom to be taken away from them, and then, on that day, they will fast."

It is clear that this text, before being taken over into an evangelical document, had originally once been handed down in isolation. It is also clear that it was eminently suited to clarify the practice of fasting. Martin Dibelius (1883–1947), the founder of New Testament form criticism, therefore took the position that texts of this kind had been handed down as samples of preaching before they were incorporated into a Gospel. He calls this form of concise, instructive story with a saying of Jesus at its heart, accordingly, a paradigm (=example-narrative).[7] His thesis, to be sure, has been in dispute even up to the present, but the possibility that original Christian preaching could have formed the setting of these stories cannot be summarily rejected.

Now we must indeed not fall into the foolish assumption that the original context of all biblical forms was liturgy. Behind the Bible stand many other, different institutions, which produced their own genres and forms. If you open the Old Testament wisdom literature, for example, you come upon comprehensive collections of proverbs and compilations of rules for life and education. You might read there:

> The lips of the king utter oracles,
>> he does not err when he speaks in judgment.
>> [PROVERBS 16:10]

48

Better an equable man than a hero,
   a man master of himself than one who takes a city;
                    [PROVERBS 16:32]

To retort without first listening
   is folly to work one's own confusion.
                    [PROVERBS 18:13]

A man finds bread sweet when it is got by fraud,
   but later his mouth is full of grit.
                    [PROVERBS 20:17]

Weigh your plans in consultation,
   with sound guidance wage your war.
                    [PROVERBS 20:18]

Such statements naturally do not arise from liturgy. Nor are they simply freely circulating proverbs used by the people when occasion warrants. The setting may be defined more accurately: The quoted sayings were used by ancient Israel in instruction, specifically for future officials and diplomats of the royal court. They were school texts, upon which writing and reading exercises were based; at the same time, however, aristocratic children at the royal court with the assistance of these texts learned the art of government, good manners, and courtly behavior.

The original purpose of Old Testament collections of proverbs shows how carefully one must judge the placement of the setting in the case of a text from ancient times. Here we must first completely lay aside our experiences and our feel for life.

Let us cite an example from a civilization closer to us in time, the courtly civilization of the Middle Ages.

Thou art mine; I am thine;
Thou canst be sure of that.
Thou art locked within my heart,
The little key is lost.
Thou shalt ever be inside.

If we had to determine the setting of this love song only by our emotions, we would probably say that it is a poem which a lover wrote to his girl friend and sent to her or recited to her at an opportune moment. The setting then would be the private relationship between two lovers.

As a matter of fact this interpretation would completely miss the point. A medieval love song was composed exclusively for the purpose of being sung aloud at a court festival, in the presence of everyone, usually in competition with other poets. So it was directed to an individual woman—but she

The literary genre *fairy tale* had its original setting in a now-vanished way of life. The wintertime spinning rooms of earlier centuries no longer exist. The new children's "storyteller" is television.

was married, and the partner in a cultivated, exquisitely refined courtly game, to which the husband listened with flattered attention, and which brought the singer the sweet sound of the chink of gold. Here too then the setting is not the private realm of the individual but a social institution.

Smiliar things could be demonstrated about many genres and forms of the past, as for example the saga, recited in the evening at the family hearth, or the fairy tale, which presumes the presence of a winter spinning room, or the ancient drama, whose origin lay in the religious festivals of the Greek city-states.

Examples of love song, saga, fairy tale, and ancient drama show very clearly that the setting of earlier genres and forms was clearly in most cases a fixed social institution. But what happened when these institutions gradually decayed and disappeared? The time of courtly palaces, of spinning rooms and tellers of sagas, even more the time of the ancient Greek religious festivals, has long since completely disappeared. Have the literary forms once produced by these far-off civilizations and institutions perished with the institutions themselves?

In the saga this is indeed the case. The feeling for tribe and clan, the connection with ancestors, and above all the way of· experiencing history presupposed by the saga, have passed from us irrevocably. The frenzied efforts of the Nazis made this quite clear. Perhaps, from Romanticism until the end of Nazism, there was something like a weak revivification of the saga. But that too is finished. The genre of saga is dead today. A modern poet could not write a saga anymore, even if he wanted to. The very fact that he would have to set it down in writing is in itself a giveaway.

But in the case of the love song the situation is different. The form in which these songs were composed has been further cultivated down to our own day. The linguistic form in this case has detached itself from the courtly institution of its origin. In Goethe's time it was already possible for a love song to be composed not for any specific circle of listeners but for unknown men and women readers of a literary periodical.

The same thing is true of drama. Ancient Greece, to be sure, has perished. The festival of Dionysus is celebrated in Athens no longer. But the *form* of the drama is alive and well. Even in the bourgeois society of the nineteenth century it experienced a vigorous florescence. But now it was performed in luxurious theaters before audiences that for the most part had no idea at all anymore about its religious origin.

And what about the fairy tale? The time of the fairy tale seems also to have passed. The phonograph record cannot replace grandmother telling fairy stories. Yet the genre of fairy tale is not really dead. It continues to live among writers who consciously use this form to illuminate or caricature present occurrences. In just such cases the external form of the fairy tale is very

The genre *drama* has received a completely new setting (*Sitz im Leben*). Originally drama was the religious mystery play of the ancient Greek city-states.

carefully preserved, but the purpose of telling it, the basic intent of the language of the fairy tale, and the audience for whom it is told have completely changed.

This all demonstrates clearly how various the fate of a linguistic form can be. It can be that it does not survive the demise of the institution which gave it a raison d'être—as, for example, the saga. Or it can be that it detaches itself from its origin and finds a new institution, it changes its setting, so to speak—examples: the love song, ancient drama. But it can also be that a specific form is consciously applied for another purpose and a different audience—as in the epic fairy tales of J. R. R. Tolkien. Here too we must speak of a change in setting.

The considerations here brought forward in regard to the love song, saga, fairy tale, and drama are of the greatest importance in relation to the Bible. Whenever a priest prays Psalm 122 as he reads his breviary ("How I rejoiced when they said to me, 'Let us go to the house of Yahweh!'"), he is saying a very ancient Jewish processional song, sung as one approached the temple in yearly pilgrimage or when one had reached the precincts of the temple. Jesus too may well have sung this song when he made the pilgrimage to Jerusalem with his parents. How the setting has changed here—from the jubilant song of the pilgrims to the silent prayer of the breviary! The only thing to remind us of the old setting would be the priest walking to and fro as he recites the prayer. Thus, easily, numberless examples could be cited. Almost all Old Testament texts obtain a new setting when we use them today. For the institutions of Israel, their original context, have perished.

But it can also be that even within the Bible itself the setting of a particular genre gradually changed or even was deliberately altered. For example, there is the Old Testament funeral song. It was intoned at the bier of the deceased by professional mourning women, but also by relatives and friends. The rhythms of these songs, their language, which was pure lamentation, the flutes that accompanied the songs, and the shrieks of the mourners formed an unmistakable unity in themselves. Their setting is clear. It couldn't be clearer. Typical for the generic style of the funeral song is the exclamation "Oh, how . . ." at the beginning or in the middle of the song. One of the greatest, most moving examples of the genre is the funeral song sung by David for Saul and Jonathan when they fell in battle against the Philistines. At the same time it is one of the oldest writings preserved from the literature of Israel.

> Alas, the glory of Israel has been slain on your heights!
> How did the heroes fall?

Do not speak of it in Gath,
nor announce it in the streets of Ashkelon,
or the daughters of the Philistines will rejoice,
the daughters of the uncircumcised will gloat.

O mountains of Gilboa,
let there be no rain or dew on you;
treacherous fields.
for there the hero's shield was dishonored!

The shield of Saul was anointed not with oil
but with blood of the wounded, fat of the warriors;
the bow of Jonathan did not turn back,
nor the sword of Saul return idle.

Saul and Jonathan, loved and lovely,
neither in life, nor in death, were divided.
Swifter than eagles were they,
stronger were they than lions.

O daughters of Israel, weep for Saul
who clothed you in scarlet and fine linen,
who set brooches of gold
on your garments.

How did the heroes fall
in the thick of the battle?

O Jonathan, in your death I am stricken,
I am desolate for you, Jonathan my brother.
Very dear to me you were,
your love to me more wonderful
than the love of a woman.

How did the heroes fall
and the battle armor fail?

[2 SAMUEL 1:19–27]

Now we can trace within the Old Testament how this pervasive and sharply outlined genre of the funeral song from the time of the great prophets could also be used for an entirely different purpose: mockery and scorn. The funeral song became a song of derision.

The most famous example of this is Isaiah 14:4–21. A prophet (Isaiah?) intones a funeral song for a great foreign king, whose name is not mentioned. But it must have been a quite specific Babylonian or Assyrian

Mourning women on the sarcophagus of King Ahiram of Byblos. They accompany their lament with gestures of grief. (*Photo courtesy of Musée National, Beirut, Lebanon.*)

54

king—a representative of the two world powers then, under whose domination Israel had to suffer so infinitely much. The song first describes how all the world breathes a sigh of relief and breaks into jubilation at the news of the death of this despot. Then there is a picture of the arrival of the deceased in the underworld and his greeting there by the inhabitants of the realm of the dead—with, mind you, a funeral song. So we have before us a funeral song within a funeral song—double derision!

One must imagine how the song was sung in the rhythm of the real lament for the dead, in the presence of a great throng of listeners. One must further imagine that the king for whom lamentation was thus being arranged was still alive and well in order to grasp the bitter scorn of it all. We can hardly estimate what effect a funeral song for a living person would have upon people of that time. For them the spoken word was a much more full and intense reality than for us. The right word in the right spot was an effective strength. If a funeral song was intoned for a living person, that just meant that he would now certainly die.

Is it not clear how much of its striking effect this song received from its close imitation of the form of the funeral song? But in reality it was after all a song of derision; even more: a cutting prophecy which foretold the imminent death of the great king. Here then we have a drastic example of a conscious alteration of the setting of a specific form—and within the Bible itself!

What was the end of the tyrant?
What was the end of his arrogance?
Yahweh has broken the staff of the wicked
and the scepter of tyrants—
which angrily thrashed the peoples
with blow after blow,
which furiously tyrannized over the nations,
persecuting without respite.
The whole earth is at rest, it is calm,
shouting for joy.
The cypresses, the cedars of Lebanon
rejoice at your fate,
"Now that you have been laid low,
no one comes up to fell us."

On your account Sheol beneath us
is astir to greet your arrival.
To honor you he rouses the ghosts
of all the rulers of the world.
He makes all the kings of the nations
get up from their thrones.

Each has something to say
and what they will say to you is this,
"So you too have been brought to nothing, like ourselves,
You too have become like us.
Your magnificence has been flung down to Sheol
with the music of your harps;
underneath you a bed of maggots,
and over you a blanket of worms.
How did you come to fall from the heavens,
Daystar, son of Dawn?
How did you come to be thrown to the ground,
you who enslaved the nations?
You who used to think to yourself,
'I will climb up to the heavens;
and higher than the stars of God
I will set my throne.
I will sit on the mount of assembly
in the recesses of the north.
I will climb to the top of thunderclouds,
I will rival the Most High.'
What! Now you have fallen to Sheol
to the very bottom of the abyss!"

[ISAIAH 14:4–15]

Such processes, in which a commonly used form was taken over but given an entirely new function, are not at all rare in the Bible. We shall see that Jesus too in his preaching took over old familiar forms for a new purpose, thus completely altering them.

In general the taking over of fixed forms with a conscious alteration of their function—that means, after all, their setting—is a much more common occurrence than we suspect. A few years ago some students in Portugal circulated a flyer with a provocative statement about Jesus, to the effect that he was a lot different than you think. He doesn't let himself be taken over by your bourgeois fascist society. He was an outsider. And if he lived among us today, he would be an outsider again. He would be haled into court as he was then. But the students wrote this not in theoretical form but in the form of a warrant:

Relevant information is requested toward the arrest of one Jesus Christ, accused of seduction, anarchical tendencies, conspiracy against the power of the state.
Special distinguishing marks: Scars on hands and feet.
Presumed profession: Carpenter.
Nationality: Jew.
Aliases: Son of Man, Prince of Peace, Light of the World.

No fixed domicile.
The person sought preaches equality of all men, advocates Utopian ideas, and must be labelled a dangerous rebel.
All pertinent information should be reported to local police.[8]

In literature too we encounter numerous cases in which familiar genres and forms are applied to a purpose which is intrinsically alien to them, and thus their original setting is completely changed. Thus Goethe, for example, gave his novel *The Sorrows of Young Werther*, which made him famous overnight, the form of a collection of documents.

The novel begins with an editor's note. The editor asserts that he has collected all the documents about the story of poor Werther that he could find, and is now presenting this collection to the reader. The novel itself consists largely of letters arranged in chronological order. Only toward the end does the editor intrude somewhat more forcibly, where he interjects the following:

> I wish that we had so many documents by his own hand about our friend's memorable last days that I did not need to interrupt the sequence of his letters by a connecting narrative. I have felt it my duty to collect accurate information from persons well acquainted with his history. The story is simple; and all accounts agree, except for some unimportant particulars. Only with respect to the character of the persons involved do opinions and judgments vary. All that is left to do, then, is to relate conscientiously the facts which our persistent labor has enabled us to collect, to give the letters found after his death, and to pay attention to even the slightest fragment from his pen, especially since it is so difficult to discover the true and innermost motives of men who are not of the common run.[9]

This text alone shows very clearly that *Werther* in its external form is a collection of documents with notes and closing remarks of the editor. The external form, however, is deceptive. Actually this is a novel. In this example we have perfect proof that the description of an external form alone does not suffice for form criticism. The function of a form and its respective setting must be determined. And we must always bear in mind that a form can be applied for entirely opposite purposes, that it can be played with, that it can receive an altogether new function and an altogether new setting.

What has been said must suffice for general considerations of the problems and working methods of form criticism. Before we turn exclusively to the fixed forms and genres of the Bible, another terminological comment is in order. The attentive reader will long ago have ascertained that the con-

Die Leiden

des

jungen Werthers.

Erster Theil.

Leipzig,
in der Weygandschen Buchhandlung.
1774.

Goethe's *The Sorrows of Young Werther* purports to be a collection of documents but is in reality a novel. The exterior form of a text and its function or, as the case may be, its setting (*Sitz im Leben*) must be very carefully distinguished. (*Title page reproduced from an edition in the Württembergische Landesbibliotheck, Stuttgart.*)

cepts of *form* and *genre* have often been used without differentiation in juxtaposition. In this is reflected a terminological problem of contemporary literary scholarship. A great number of scholars make no distinction at all between form and genre. Others call the smaller units "forms," and the large units such as the novel or drama "genres." A third group of scholars calls the structure of a single, individual text "form" and typical forms which frequently recur "genres." According to the terminology of this third group, we would have had to speak of "genre criticism" almost everywhere that we have used the term "form criticism" in this book. Unfortunately literary scholars, as is so often the case with scholars in general, have not yet agreed about their terminology. And since the expression "form criticism" is still applied in almost every instance in a comprehensive sense (also then in the sense of genre criticism) it cannot here be suppressed.

III

FIXED FORMS IN THE BIBLE

— 1 —

The Multitude of Biblical Genres and Forms

Normally books contain only one single genre. If you go into a bookstore and buy Thomas Mann's *Buddenbrooks*, you get a book which is a novel and nothing else from start to finish. Or if you prefer to purchase a *History of the United States*, you get a book which is historical writing and nothing else from start to finish. And if you go to a music store and buy a volume of Schubert's songs, you'll find a song collection in that book and very surely nothing else.

A book in which *Buddenbrooks*, a *History of the United States*, and a collection of Schubert's songs are printed, one after the other, just doesn't exist. Can one then reason that a book always, without exception, contains a single literary genre? No, this reasoning would be wrong.

We need only to open the pages of the "Collected Works" of a great writer—if possible in a compact, one-volume edition—to see at once that there are exceptions. Perhaps we would encounter in one volume such varied genres as novel, verse epic, drama, novella, poem, aphorism, and letter. Just the same, in this case all the texts, however varied the genres to which they belong, have one thing in common: They all come from the same literary genius, indeed perhaps are even, as Goethe said of his works. "fragments of a single, great confession."

There are books, however, in which not only are extremely varied literary genres and forms contained but also quite different authors speak to us. A good example is the reader or anthology used in secondary and higher education, or the old McGuffey Readers. Often they are like a colorful mosaic. When I take my old secondary-school reader down from my bookshelf, I find in the first part—along with much other material—the Lord's Prayer from the Gothic Bible, aphoristic wisdom from the *Edda*, Germanic magical incantations, a fragment from the *Lay of Hildebrand*. an Icelandic saga, a part of the *Song of the Nibelungs*, love poetry, a text from the Limburg Chronicle, a section of a law book (*Mirror of the Saxons*), a Mardi Gras play by Hans Sachs, samples from Luther's Bible translation, poems from the Baroque, passages from Christoph von Grimmelshausen's *Simplicissimus*, and a wedding homily from Abraham a Sancta Clara.

How many centuries, how many authors, how many different genres are here expressed? A whole list of genres could be set up on the basis of the table of contents: prayer, homily, edifying tract, saying, proverb, saga, droll tale, legal decision, chronicle, song, poem. Such a diversity of authors and genres is possible only in a book in which very diverse literature is compiled from diverse periods of time.

But the Bible is just such a book as this. In the Bible there is a collection of texts from many centuries, from many authors, and from the most varied genres. There are the four Gospels, there are letters and collections of letters, there are books of prophecy and documents of revelation, instructional writings and books of wisdom; there is a whole hymnal—namely, a collection of 150 psalms—and finally there are the so-called historical books. To be sure, this term should be avoided, for the historical books of the Bible are not historical in the modern sense.

These, in essence, are the genres of the books of the Bible. But it is very important to note that these large genres contain within themselves the most varied smaller genres. Thus modern exegesis distinguishes in the Bible between historical account, saga, myth, fairy tale, fable, paradigm, homily, admonition, confession, instructive narrative, similitude, parable, illustrative saying, prophetic utterance, juridical saying, wise saying, proverb, riddle, speech, contract, list, prayer, song.

And this list is by no means exhaustive. Form-critical studies of the last few decades have discovered a far greater number of fixed genres in the Bible and are constantly discovering more. Above all, most of the genres listed can be further differentiated. Thus, in the Book of Psalms there are quite different kinds of songs. We find there hymns, songs of lamentation, and songs of thanksgiving, which even by their form alone are quite distinct from one another. Other genres of song are found outside the Psalter: songs of derision, battle songs, victory songs, funeral songs, wedding songs, and love songs. In similar fashion one or the other of the genres listed above could be further differentiated.

One must actually say that the book we call the Bible contains an almost limitless abundance of the most varied genres and forms. Moreover, it is not only the great number of these various genres which is remarkable but also how varied they are and how variously they express reality. We have seen that there is no modern book in which is printed in one volume a novel, a historical essay, and a collection of songs. But the Bible does unite

In earlier school Bibles the wonderful, colorful variety of the biblical forms was forced into the narrow mold of "Bible history."

in itself such opposites. Or can forms of human discourse be imagined which would be more vividly in contrast to each other than the Book of Jonah, the succession history of David, the Wisdom of the Preacher, the words of the Apocalypse of St. John, or the love poetry of the Song of Songs?

Unfortunately past centuries have been unable to see the colorful abundance of forms which the Bible contains. As a matter of fact, only three genres of biblical books were recognized: histories, instructional books, and prophecies. This superficial, mechanical division caused Tobit to be assigned to the histories, Jonah to the prophets, and the Psalter to the instructional books. If only the differences between these three categories had been taken seriously! But in reality it was even worse: The so-called historical books were extolled and raised into disproportionate attention. The Bible was steamrollered into *Bible history*.

To illustrate this point one has only to glance at the old Ecker Bible, which up to 1957 was used for Catholic religious instruction in Germany. The instructional and prophetic books, in relation to the "history" books, are here forced completely into the background. Only Messianic texts have been selected from the prophets, and even these are set in small type. And the "history" books? They serve as a quarry for a continuous presentation of history into which even books such as Job, Jonah, Tobit, and Daniel are somehow forced. But the worst thing is that in this continuous presentation of history there are passages which do not occur in the Bible at all! There they stand, with no special note or apology, among real biblical texts and thus intensify the impression that the Bible presents a connected, unified, rounded-off presentation of history. As an example, the Ecker Bible concludes its version of the Acts of the Apostles as follows:

> (5. Paul comes to Rome.) After three months they journeyed further. When they arrived in *Rome*, Paul was allowed to move into a house of his own, except that he was guarded by a soldier. He remained in these rented quarters two full years, and received all who came to him. He preached the kingdom of God and explained the teachings of the Lord Jesus Christ with freedom of spirit and unimpeded.
>
> After two years of imprisonment the Apostle was released from confinement. Then he undertook a new journey of conversion, which lasted two years. First he went to Spain. Then from there he turned again to the East to visit the congregations in Ephesus, Crete, Macedonia, and Miletus. Finally, in the reign of the Emperor Nero he came back to Rome again. There, in A.D. 67, he suffered the death of a martyr: As a Roman citizen he was beheaded.[10]

The Ecker Bible with this text evokes the impression of telling the story of the Bible in its own words. But in reality only the first passage of the text cited can claim the Bible as authority. Luke's Acts does actually contain these words:

> Paul spent the whole of the two years in his own rented lodging. He welcomed all who came to visit him, proclaiming the kingdom of God and teaching the truth about the Lord Jesus Christ with complete freedom and without hindrance from anyone.
>
> [ACTS 28:30–31]

But this sentence ends the Book of Acts. The Bible says nothing about what Ecker records in the second part. This all sprang from the imagination of later Christians. Paul never went to Spain or to the East but was executed in Rome after his imprisonment. Luke knew that, by the way, but does not record it, because he wasn't interested in telling the story of Paul or even of the apostles. His aim was solely to present the origin and growth of the Church, up to Paul's arrival in Rome. So he could close his account fittingly at that point. Enough of this example! But we could name many others.

The dreadful thing about the methodology of this old school Bible is not only that it mixes extrabiblical vignettes of "history" with biblical texts, but above all that it in no way concerns itself with the genre and basic intent of each book of the Bible. The whole Bible, with its innumerable genres and forms, is ground up into a uniform "Bible history." The level and purpose of the individual biblical author's presentation of history is ignored. And "history" in the Bible does not always mean "report of historically determinable data." This fact is even more flagrantly ignored. But perhaps one should not reproach the old Ecker Bible too severely for all these misleading errors. The time was not yet ripe for a careful, discriminating consideration of biblical genres.

Today, to be sure, no interpretation of the Bible can disregard the fact that in this book we are addressed in a variety of genres and forms. It is of course impossible in the space of this book to go into every biblical genre. But let us at least select the most important of them, so as to obtain a better approach to the way the Bible speaks.

2

The Poor Man's Lamb

Let us begin with the genre of the similitude, for this is the one in which we can learn much about the Bible's way of expressing reality. Let us choose for our point of departure a similitude of Jesus, the familiar story of the sower. In Mark's version it reads like this:

> "Listen! Imagine a sower going out to sow. Now it happened that, as he sowed, some of the seed fell on the edge of the path, and the birds came and ate it up. Some seed fell on rocky ground where it found little soil and sprang up straightaway, because there was no depth of earth; and when the sun came up it was scorched and, not having any roots, it withered away. Some seed fell into thorns, and the thorns grew up and choked it, and it produced no crop. And some seeds fell into rich soil and, growing tall and strong, produced crop; and yielded thirty, sixty, even a hundredfold." And he said, "Listen, anyone who has ears to hear!"
>
> [MARK 4:3–9]

Before we turn to the form of this similitude, let us first comment on its content. For European or American circumstances the similitude is not understandable. What sower in Europe or America would have been so foolish as to sow seed on the footpath, over the rocks, and among thorns? But in ancient Palestine this was quite the order of the day, for there sowing was done not after plowing, as we do, but before. "The sower of the similitude then walks across the unplowed field of stubble. Now it is understandable why he sows on the footpath: He strews his seed intentionally on the path the villagers have trodden across the field of stubble, because it too is to be plowed under. Intentionally also he drops seed on the thorns, which stand withered on the fallow field, because they too are to be plowed under. And it is no longer surprising that seed falls upon the rocks; the limestone rocks are covered with a thin crust of soil and project hardly (or not at all) above the field of stubble, before the plowshare, with a grating sound, collides with them. What appears to Westerners as lack of skill turns out to be ordinary procedure under Palestinian circumstances."[11]

Thus, in the similitude of the sower Jesus describes the very unfavorable conditions and difficulties which menace the farmer in Palestine in his time. He is describing things familiar at the time to every agricultural laborer. And what happens at the end of the similitude was likewise known to everyone, because it had often been experienced, often like a miracle: Despite all the hostile forces of nature which threaten the destruction of the seed, despite animals, poor soil, and weeds, in the end there is an abundant harvest, some of the seed bears thirtyfold, other seed bears sixtyfold, and other seed a hundredfold.

Jesus wants to tell us in this similitude that the coming of God's kingdom is like sowing and harvest. Despite all hostile forces and difficulties which work against my preaching and my effectiveness, yes, although up to now everything appears to be hopeless, in the end the kingdom of God will be present in unexpected fullness and glory. So much for the content of the similitude. Let us now concern ourselves with its form. How can one actually recognize the narrative of the undiscouraged sower as a similitude?

First, of course, by what has immediately preceded it in Mark's Gospel:

> "He taught them many things in similitudes, and in the course of his teaching he said to them, . . ."
>
> [MARK 4:2]

Of course this comment is original with the evangelist. But we must assume that Jesus already was beginning the narrative of the sower in a form which made clear to every one of his hearers: "Now we will hear a similitude!" Perhaps the whole situation and Jesus' cadence of speech already indicated a similitude; perhaps, however, Jesus used a special opening formula which designated the narrative to follow as a similitude. In any case, we have preserved for us a whole set of such opening formulas for his similitudes—for example:

> "What can we say that the kingdom of God is like? What similitude can we find for it? It is like a mustard seed, which . . ."
>
> [MARK 4:30–31]

or, more briefly,

> "What shall I compare the kingdom of God with? It is like the yeast . . ."
>
> [LUKE 13:20–21]

or,

> "This is what the kingdom of God is like, a man, who . . ."
>
> [MARK 4:26]

These introductions to similitudes employ the dative case in Greek (in English, usually "to what," "with what," or "like what"). The opening can be reduced to the formula "I want to tell you a similitude. With what can we compare the thing we want to discuss? It is like a . . ."

Another way in which Jesus began similitudes was the question form, which, for example, would look like this:

> "Or, again, what woman with ten drachmas would not, if she lost one, light a lamp and sweep the house and search thoroughly till she found it? And then, when she had found it, call together her friends and neighbors? 'Rejoice with me,' she would say, 'I have found the drachma I lost.'"
>
> [LUKE 15:8–9]

When the narrative began thus as a question, the hearers knew at once that here too they were about to hear a similitude.

But not all of Jesus' similitudes begin with the dative case or a question. The similitude of the sower, for example, begins very simply and neatly: "A sower went out to sow." The principal figure of the similitude then is in the nominative case at the beginning, and the whole thing starts like an ordinary narrative. Many biblical stories begin according to the pattern of this opening. This category is called "Similitudes with nominative beginning." Examples:

> "A man was once on his way from Jerusalem to Jericho . . ."
>
> [LUKE 10:30]

> "There was a man who gave a great banquet . . ."
>
> [LUKE 14:16]

> "A man had two sons . . ."
>
> [LUKE 15:11]

> "There was a rich man and he had a steward . . ."
>
> [LUKE 16:1]

> "There was a rich man who used to dress in purple . . ."
>
> [LUKE 16:19]

> "Two men went up to the Temple . . ."
>
> [LUKE 18:10]

When a story began in the nominative case and launched its narrative without any preparation, hearers in the ancient Near East could assume with a certain confidence that they were about to hear a similitude.

"In the same town were two men . . ."

[2 SAMUEL 12:1]

"There was a judge in a certain town . . ."

[LUKE 18:2]

Of course this way of beginning similitudes is also formulaic. If a narrative began in this way, with a subject noun right at the beginning and with a plot which has no long buildup but comes to the point at once, the listener could assume with a certain security that he would hear a similitude.

Can we determine from the similitude of the sower still more signs which make a narrative *formally* recognizable as a similitude? There is at least one which must not be overlooked: Although the entire similitude is told as a story, as something that happened to a specific sower as he once sowed his seed, it nonetheless describes from the first to last sentence only typical and everyday occurrences. It tells of sowing, the fate of the crop, the threat to the seed, the abundance of the harvest.

This is true of many of Jesus' similitudes. They speak of universally familiar circumstances, everywhere found, constantly and always repeated. They speak of the growth of seed, of weeds in the wheat, of fermented dough, of fish in the net, of building towers and waging war, of children playing, of the joy of finding lost money, of discovering secret treasure, of what happens to a sterile fig tree. These are all things which happen every day, whose laws of operation are known to everyone. From this very point a similitude receives its argumentative power: No one can dispute the everyday workings of nature.

A characteristic of Jesus' similitudes then, is that they relate typical, everyday events. This is how we recognize them. Furthermore, this is also the strongest reason why Jesus' parables are so short and concise: A narrator does not have to describe at length occurrences which repeat themselves regularly and with which everyone is familiar. It is often enough for him to remind his hearers of them with a single sentence.

Jesus also, however, tells similitudes in which unusual or even unique situations are recounted rather than typical, everyday occurrences. Thus, for example, in the similitude of the great banquet:

"There was a man who gave a great banquet, and he invited a large number of people. When the time for the banquet came, he sent his servant to say to those who had been invited, 'Come along, everything is ready now.' But all alike started to make excuses. The first said, 'I have bought a piece of land, and must go and see it. Please accept my apologies.' Another said, 'I have bought five yoke of oxen and am on my way to try them out. Please accept my apologies.' Yet another said, 'I have just got married and so am unable to come.'

The servant returned and reported this to his master. Then the householder, in a rage, said to his servant, 'Go out quickly into the streets and alleys of the town and bring in here the poor, the crippled, the blind and the lame.' 'Sir,' said the servant, 'your orders have been carried out, and there is still room.' Then the master said to his servant, 'Go into the open roads and the hedgerows and force people to come in to make sure my house is full; because, I tell you, not one of those who were invited shall have a taste of my banquet.' "

[LUKE 14:16–24]

In this similitude also everything goes according to rule and the way the hearers might expect. A man gives a big party and a long while ahead of time invites guests. According to the custom of aristocratic Jerusalem circles he then sends out, just before the dinner, a second invitation. And now the unexpected thing, the unpleasant surprise, happens. All those who have been invited, who have already accepted, give excuses for not coming. Each one has a reason for staying away. Not one comes. An unusual situation! It impels the host to act in an unusual manner. He invites the poor and homeless of the town, and does not rest until the last place at table is taken. One must picture the scene: a house full of cripples, ragged tramps, and vagrants! What the host does is illuminating in its way. His behavior is understandable, but the whole thing is indeed extraordinary.

Everyone at once realizes that this is a very different form of narrative than the similitude of the sower. Biblical scholarship has a special term for similitudes of this second kind, in which neither typical nor everyday occurrences, but extraordinary, even unique occurrences are described. Such similitudes are called *parables*—for example, the similitudes of the prodigal son (Luke 15:11–32), the kind employer (Matthew 20:1–16), the unmerciful servant (Matthew 18:23–35), the crooked steward (Luke 16:1–8), and the wicked tenants (Mark 12:1–11).

Just because the parable operates with unusual rather than ordinary situations, it is more difficult than the similitude (in the strict sense) to recognize as a similitude. How for example can one tell that in the narrative of the great banquet we are dealing formally with a similitude and not a factual report?

First of all there is the nominative beginning of the narrative: "A man arranged a great banquet. . . ." It is not said who the man is, where he lives, or when and where he gave his party. What is said is only: "A man gave a big party and invited many guests." Of course the oriental listener pricked up his ears at such a beginning. He probably suspected that a similitude was about to be told.

Even in the actual narrative, despite the uniqueness of the narrated content, much is still schematized. The first errand of the messenger, in any case long and circumstantial, in which he has had to memorize the most varied excuses, has been condensed to a single scene, in which three of the guests, representing the rest, excuse themselves. After this the parable describes in two scenes, again carefully stylized, how the banquet room is filled. And the fact that in the whole story only one servant appears, who has to do everything, is naturally also narrative technique: In reality there would have been several servants in attendance at that place and that time. This artistic simplification of the thread of narrative, which is simultaneously a dramatization of the content, is typical for all biblical similitudes and especially for parables. Jesus' auditors accordingly probably would know, in the case of a parable, that a similitude was being told. They would receive no ultimate guarantee that this was so, however, for this technique of narration also existed at the time in other narrative genres.

Whoever heard the parable of the great banquet was sure that it was a similitude either from the start—by the way it began—or later, at the moment when the parable was finished and the listener directly addressed. In Luke this revelation to the hearer is accomplished by the change from singular to plural. Up to this point it was always the servant who was addressed. But now Jesus says, "But I tell *you* [plural] not one of those who were invited shall have a taste of my banquet." Who is speaking here? Jesus himself or the householder? The question is not so easy to decide. But it is certain in any case that it is only with this sentence that the narrative has been revealed as a similitude or a parable.

I hope then it has been made plain that a parable is much harder to differentiate from an ordinary narrative than is an actual similitude. Of course the narrators of that time were aware of this. They frequently made profitable use of the similarity and consciously narrated a parable disguised as a factual report. A most celebrated example is the parable of the poor man's lamb, which the prophet Nathan tells to King David in the Second Book of Samuel.

The context is familiar: David has seduced Bathsheba, wife of Uriah the Hittite, while Uriah is fighting a war for him. In order to escape the consequences, David maliciously causes Uriah to be murdered and marries Bathsheba. Then the prophet Nathan comes to David and tells him this story:

> "In the same town were two men,
>   one rich, the other poor.
>   The rich man had flocks and herds
>   in great abundance;
>   the poor man had nothing but a ewe lamb,
>   one only, a small one he had bought.
>   This he fed, and it grew up with him and his children,

eating his bread, drinking from his cup,
sleeping on his breast; it was like a daughter to him.
When there came a traveller to stay, the rich man
refused to take one of his own flock or herd
to provide for the wayfarer who had come to him.
Instead he took the poor man's lamb
and prepared it for his guest."

[2 SAMUEL 12:1–4]

David is furious when he has heard the tale. He says to Nathan:

"As Yahweh lives . . . the man who did this deserves to die! He must make fourfold restitution for the lamb, for doing such a thing and showing no compassion."
Then Nathan said to David, "You are the man."

[2 SAMUEL 12:5–7]

The tale gives a most exact description of David's meanness and inhumanity to Uriah. After all, David had not only appropriated the wife of one of his most loyal followers; at this time he had already a whole harem at his disposal. Yet David does not notice how Nathan's tale unmasks David himself. Why is he so imperceptive? Probably because the tale is not at all readily recognizable as a similitude, but reported in such a way as to make one think that some rich man somewhere in the country actually did rob his poor neighbor of a lamb.

The opening, "Two men lived in a city" (nominative beginning), shows to the knowledgeable listener that now a similitude might be coming. Furthermore, in a genuine report, at least the name of the city would necessarily be recorded. Also, the carefully stylized description of the manner in which the poor man treats the lamb causes us to listen carefully and think of the possibility of a similitude. On the other hand, the behavior of the rich man is so sordid and infamous that again one is inclined to believe this to be a concrete, actual event.

So there can be no doubt: This passage is a combination of two different narrative genres. Nathan tells a story which consciously blurs the distinction between report and parable. He plays with the report form and gives it the function of a parable. David could certainly see that what he is hearing is a parable, and that it is about himself. But on the other hand the story is so exciting and unusual that he is carried away and drawn into the linguistic play of the tale. This is just what Nathan intends.

And probably all parables have the same intention. It would really be worth investigating to see whether every parable does not originally toy with the genre of the report, that is, whether the narrator of the parable does not at first consciously leave open whether he is reporting an actual occurrence

Nathan deliberately plays with the parable form. He tells a story that wobbles between report and parable. Thus David does not notice that he himself is intended.

or narrating a similitude. The listener is supposed to be utterly spellbound by the story, so that he forgets the present and can closely identify himself with the situation in the story. Only at the end does it dawn on him: He means *me!* He's talking about my personal situation!

Did Jesus also tell his parables like those about the great banquet, the prodigal son, or the malicious tenants in this way? Did he also often consciously leave his hearers for a while uncertain as to whether he is narrating a similitude or an actual occurrence? This we can hardly now determine with certainty. But we may assume it, for the Gospels show that Jesus employed the genres of the similitude and the parable in a most masterly fashion.

All this clearly demonstrates that there are similitudes which can be recognized even by their beginning or the typology of their content as similitudes. But there are also others which at first conceal their genre; they consciously play with the form of the *report* and can only be identified as similitudes by their situation and accompanying circumstances.

After preliminary considerations about the form of similitudes we are now ready for the question of most interest to us: What is the relationship of the similitude to historical reality?

The question is justified, for the similitude after all tells a story. Often it tells the story with great excitement and drama. Sometimes it is so exciting that at first glance one could think that real events were being narrated. The similitude of the sower, for example, is not the least bit concerned with describing the concrete experiences of a specific sower who lived somewhere in Palestine. And the parable of the great banquet does not have the least intention of reporting the background and circumstances of a real banquet. And even the parable of the poor man's lamb does not intend to state categorically that somewhere in the country a live lamb was stolen. The truth of this similitude then does not lie on the level of pure factuality. That is, a similitude is not designed to communicate historical data that correspond in every respect to the narrative of the similitude.

And yet all biblical similitudes are somewhat concerned with history. The similitude of the sower speaks of an actual happening: how the kingdom of God, despite all opposition, keeps increasing and coming to us as an abundant harvest. The parable of the great banquet represents a real event: God is on the point of inviting Israel to the great eschatological banquet; if his invitation is refused, he will invite someone else. The parable of the poor man's sheep, above all, sheds light on events which really took place—namely, what David did to Uriah. That's the way it is with all biblical similitudes. They neither report historical occurrences corresponding to the action of the similitude nor preach general religious ideas, but in their imagery they cast light on events that are actually happening or have already happened. Finally, then, the biblical similitudes speak of a real event, but they narrate this event not on the historical level but figuratively.

Not only similitudes but many other narrative forms of the Bible operate in the same way. In the following pages we will repeatedly encounter the fact that biblical stories can, to be sure, present things with plasticity and lucidity, but they are often not at all or not primarily concerned with a sequence of external events but rather with a deeper lying reality.

Everyone realizes this in the case of a similitude. With other narrative genres of the Bible this insight appears to be more difficult—as, for example, in the case of the genre of the instructive narrative. Let us now discuss this.

———— 3 ————————————————

Jonah and His God

Probably the greatest example of an instructive narrative is the Book of Jonah. If one ventures to relate its plot or summarize its content, one is sure, after a series of unsuccessful attempts, to come to the conclusion that it won't work. This is a most concise, condensed, and artistic narrative. It is a document intended to instruct—the didactic tendency is unmistakable—and yet all the didacticism is raised to the level of pure artistic narration. Since every sentence is important, let us quote it here virtually in full:

> The word of Yahweh was addressed to Jonah son of Amittai: "Up!" he said, "Go to Nineveh, the great city, and inform them that their wickedness has become known to me." Jonah decided to run away from Yahweh, and to go to Tarshish. He went down to Joppa and found a ship bound for Tarshish; he paid his fare and went aboard, to go with them to Tarshish, to get away from Yahweh. But Yahweh unleashed a violent wind on the sea, and there was such a great storm at sea that the ship threatened to break up. The sailors took fright, and each of them called on his own god, and to lighten the ship they threw the cargo overboard. Jonah, however, had gone below and lain down in the hold and fallen fast asleep. The boatswain came upon him and said, "What do you mean by sleeping? Get up! Call upon your god! Perhaps he will spare us a thought, and not leave us to die." Then they said to each other, "Come on, let us draw lots to find out who is responsible for bringing this evil on us." So they cast lots, and the lot fell to Jonah.

Then they said to him, "Tell us, what is your business? Where do you come from? What is your country? What is your nationality?" He replied, "I am a Hebrew, and I worship Yahweh, the God of heaven, who made the sea and the land." The sailors were seized with terror at this and said, "What have you done?" They knew that he was trying to escape from Yahweh, because he had told them so. They then said, "What are we to do with you, to make the sea grow calm for us?" For the sea was growing rougher and rougher. He replied, "Take me and throw me into the sea, and then it will grow calm for you. For I can see that it is my fault that this violent storm has happened to you." The sailors rowed hard in an effort to reach the shore, but in vain, since the sea grew still rougher for them. They then called on Yahweh and said, "O Yahweh, do not let us perish for taking this man's life; do not hold us guilty of innocent blood; for you, Yahweh, have acted as you have thought right." And taking hold of Jonah they threw him into the sea; and the sea grew calm again. At this the men were seized with dread of Yahweh; they offered a sacrifice to Yahweh and made vows.

Yahweh had arranged that a great fish should be there to swallow Jonah; and Jonah remained in the belly of the fish for three days and three nights. From the belly of the fish he prayed to Yahweh, his God. . . . Yahweh spoke to the fish, which then vomited Jonah on to the shore.

The word of Yahweh was addressed a second time to Jonah: "Up!" he said, "Go to Nineveh, the great city, and preach to them as I told you." Jonah set out and went to Nineveh in obedience to the word of Yahweh. Now Nineveh was a city great beyond compare: it took three days to cross it. Jonah went on into the city, making a day's journey. He preached in these words, "Only forty days more, and Nineveh is going to be destroyed." And the people of Nineveh believed in God; they proclaimed a fast and put on sackcloth and sat down in ashes. A proclamation was then promulgated throughout Nineveh, by decree of the king and his ministers, as follows: "Men and beasts, herds and flocks, are to taste nothing; they must not eat, they must not drink water. All are to put on sackcloth and call on God with all their might; and let everyone renounce his evil behavior and the wicked things he has done. Who knows if God will not change his mind and relent, if he will not renounce his burning wrath, so that we do not perish?" God saw their efforts to renounce their evil behavior. And God relented: he did not inflict on them the disaster which he had threatened.

Jonah was very indignant at this; he fell into a rage. He prayed to Yahweh and said, "Ah! Yahweh, is not this just as I said would happen when I was still at home? That was why I went and fled to Tarshish: I knew that you were a God of tenderness and compassion, slow to anger, rich in graciousness, relenting from evil. So now Yahweh, please take away my life, for I might as well be dead as go on living." Yahweh replied, "Are you right to be angry?" Jonah then went out of the city and sat down to the east of the city. There he made himself a shelter and sat under it in the shade, to see what would happen to the city. Then Yahweh God arranged that a castor-oil plant should grow up over Jonah to give shade for his head and soothe his ill-humor; Jonah was delighted with the castor-oil plant. But at dawn the next day, God arranged that a worm should attack the castor-oil plant—and it withered. Next, when the sun rose, God arranged that there should be a scorching east wind; the sun beat down so hard on Jonah's head that he was overcome and begged for death, saying, "I might as well be dead as go on living." God said to Jonah, "Are you right to be angry about the castor-oil plant?" He replied, "I have every right to be angry, to the point of death." Yahweh replied, "You are only upset about a castor-oil plant which cost you no labor, which you did not make grow, which sprouted in a night and has perished in a night. And am I not to feel sorry for Nineveh, a great city, in which there are more than a hundred twenty thousand people who cannot tell their right hand from their left, to say nothing of all the animals?"

[JONAH 1:1–2:2, 2:11–4:11]

The last scene, in which Jonah and God stand alone together, shows most clearly that this great narrative is didactic. One thing is obvious: This scene is not an appendix but the climax of the book. The flight of Jonah and the events in Nineveh—all this had been told only so that the premises for the final conversation between God and Jonah might be laid down. For the first time we know why Jonah fled from God, and not until now does the explanation between Jonah and God achieve its decisive phase. The conversation is opened by Jonah's frightening prayer, because he is angry at God for being merciful to Nineveh. The behavior of God is so repellent to him and strikes so deep into his soul that he would rather die than endure it. To Jonah's prayer corresponds God's great admission at the end of the scene, by far his longest speech in the entire book, in which he justifies his mercy on the city of Nineveh. Between these two speeches comes the wonderful episode of the castor-oil plant, in which God's short question forms the transition: "Are you right to be angry?"

This very arrangement illustrates the fact that this is an artistically constructed, fictive scene, intended to fascinate and instruct the reader. The direction of the whole passage toward the reader really becomes clear when it is observed that God's final speech ends with a question: "And am I not to feel sorry for Nineveh, the great city?" For a book which claims to record historical events it would be absolutely necessary to continue with Jonah's story, whether he yielded to God or persisted in his narrow selfishness. The Book of Jonah does not tell us—both possibilities are left open. It closes with a question and so makes clear that it is not Jonah who is important but the reader himself. It is the latter to whom God speaks and of whom he

Castor-oil plant, worm, and broiling sun are all essential composition elements of the last part of the narrative of Jonah. The story uses them to reach its high point.

asks the question. Thus we are forced to the conclusion that in the end Jonah is not the historical prophet Jonah at all but a condensed personalization of Jewish readers whom the author has in mind. He is concerned with stirring up his readers and making them understand that God is quite different from the way they imagine him.

This didactic element, which, to be sure, is completely masked by the story line, becomes perfectly clear when we look closely at the episode with the castor-oil plant. A whole dramatic device is here carefully staged and set in motion by God. Three times the same phrase occurs in Hebrew: "and God arranged . . ." At first God *arranges* that a castor-oil plant should grow right beside the rather pitiful leaf-shelter of Jonah. Jonah is pleased with the additional shade. Hardly has the plant attained full growth when God *arranges* for a worm to eat the plant. The plant withers; Jonah's shade is gone. Thirdly God *arranges* a scorching desert wind. Now the absence of shade takes effect. Jonah gets a headache. When one notices how lightly all this is told, and that the miniature tragedy of the castor-oil plant, the worm, and the hot wind is actually designed only to introduce the rapid swing of Jonah's mood (for he is highly sensitive and at once takes offense), then one can hardly avoid the impression that the writer has written the whole episode with barely concealed tongue in cheek. On the other hand the writer is very serious, for to Jonah's little misery the great suffering of God is to be contrasted.[12]

> "You are only upset about a castor-oil plant which cost you no labor. . . . And am I not to feel sorry for Nineveh, the great city, in which there are more than a hundred and twenty thousand people who cannot tell their right hand from their left, to say nothing of all the animals?"
>
> [JONAH 4:10–11]

It is obvious that the last scene of the Book of Jonah is a narrative fiction, emanating *in toto* from the didactic purpose of the writer. It is just the same with the whole book. The great fish, for example, has just the same function as the castor-oil plant, the worm, and the hot wind: It is supposed to bring the resistant, reluctant Jonah to the point where God wants him. Here too the same word is used as at the end of the book: God "*arranged that* a great fish . . ."

That the Book of Jonah is not intended as a historical report but as a didactic narrative is shown by one final observation: The writer works very hard with typifications. For example, the introduction of the Assyrian king is instructive. His name is not mentioned—despite the concreteness of the story; he remains colorless and indistinct; indeed he is called not even king of *Assur* as is elsewhere the custom in the Old Testament but king of

Nineveh. This makes clear that the Assyrian Empire is for the writer a grandeur of the distant past. Furthermore, for him the king of Nineveh is only a necessary puppet in the tense structure of his story: A definite historical personage of Assyria on the contrary lies completely outside his scope. He is simply not interested in recording a specific concrete event in Assyrian history.

Much the same is true of the great city of Nineveh. It can be proved that Nineveh in the time of the historical prophet Jonah, who appeared under Jeroboam II (787–47 B.C.), was by no means as yet the residential city of the Assyrian kings. Furthermore it appears almost impossible that at that time a prophet from Israel could have appeared in the capital of Assyria. But such considerations are unjust to the writer of the Book of Jonah. For he is not the least bit concerned with the historical city of Nineveh. For him Nineveh is rather a symbol for the great, powerful, and largely sinister world of paganism. He intends to speak not of God's relationship to Nineveh but of his relationship to pagans. His meaning is that God is concerned not only with Israel but also with the pagans.

That the figure of Jonah is likewise a personification, we have already seen. He represents the Jewish readers whom the writer of the book intends to address. He probably only borrowed the name from the historical prophet Jonah. Of biographical interest in the real Jonah there can be no question at all. The time of his appearance is not mentioned, his home, known from 2 Kings 14:25, is not located; not even the title "prophet" is accorded him. In his self-introduction on the ship he says of himself only that he is a Hebrew. Therefore it has with good reason been assumed that Israel itself is symbolized in Jonah's person,[13] a stubborn and self-isolating Israel always occupied with itself, evading the actual will of God, and unaware that God loves other peoples just as much as Israel itself. This is the Israel before whom the author of Jonah intends to hold the mirror. Only when one has once realized that the story of Jonah is not intended to record concrete historical events but, on the contrary, to speak of Israel and Israel's God in the form of a most perspicuous narrative, can one understand at all the individual features of the book in all their importance and wide sweep.

Let us remember for example that Jonah admits in the presence of the ship's company: "I worship Yahweh, the God of heaven, who made the sea and the land." Such a sentence, naturally, on the lips of a man who is fleeing from Yahweh, is a contradiction in itself. Jonah knows and admits that God made earth and sea; he knows, therefore, of God's omnipotence and omnipresence and yet believes that he can escape from this God on a ship. Let us reflect: In a biographical report this would be just a tragic feature in the historical prophet Jonah. If, however, we have here an instructive narrative, and if Jonah is at the same time Israel itself, then all this has a much deeper purpose. For it is vividly shown here that Israel has its confession of faith and can recite it, but significance of that confession Israel either has not yet understood or will not understand.

Or let us look at another feature of the story. How cautiously and tactfully God tries to obtain Jonah's understanding! "Are you right to be angry?" If we were reading a record of historical events, we would have to agree that at the time God was concerned about Jonah. Nothing else! But if the Book of Jonah is an instructive narrative and constantly keeps the contemporary Jewish reader in mind, then the actual meaning of this feature of the story is that God is full of cautious loving concern for his Israel, even when Israel curls up like a prickly hedgehog in its state of stubborn refusal to understand.

It has probably become apparent that only the consistent serious consideration of the narrative genre can open up the range and depth of the Book of Jonah. By a radical form criticism nothing of this book is lost. On the contrary! Its entire significance and challenging contemporaneity only now come to light.

The Book of Jonah has manifested itself from its form as an instructive narrative. It is neither historical writing nor biography. Yet it has much in common with the genre of the similitude: as in the similitude a concrete, exciting story is told which does not claim to be a historical report; its truth is on quite a different level. Like many similitudes the book ends with a question which the hearer, or in our case the reader, must answer himself. And if the writer had wished to do so, he could have ripped aside the mask of the neutral narrator at the end of the book, just as Nathan did when he confronted David, in order to exclaim, "You people of Israel, who have read this story—you yourselves are Jonah!" It is to the credit of the writer's delicate sense of style that he does no such thing but ends his narrative with the tender, humorous question of God.

— 4 —

The Saga of the Sacrifice of Isaac

Let us turn now to another narrative genre of the Bible. Let the following text serve as an example:

It happened some time later that God put Abraham to the test. "Abraham, Abraham," he called. "Here I am," he replied. "Take your son," God said, "your only son Isaac, whom you love, and go to the land of Moriah. There you shall offer him as a burnt offering, on a mountain I will point out to you."

Rising early next morning Abraham saddled his ass and took with him two of his servants and his son Isaac. He chopped wood for the burnt offering and started on his journey to the place God had pointed out to him. On the third day Abraham looked up and saw the place in the distance. Then Abraham said to his servants, "Stay here with the donkey. The boy and I will go over there; we will worship and come back to you."

Abraham took the wood for the burnt offering, loaded it on Isaac, and carried in his own hands the fire and the knife. Then the two of them set out together. Isaac spoke to his father Abraham, "Father," he said. "Yes, my son," he replied. "Look," he said "here are the fire and the wood, but where is the lamb for the burnt offering?" Abraham answered, "My son, God himself will provide the lamb for the burnt offering." Then the two of them went on together.

When they arrived at the place God had pointed out to him, Abraham built an altar there, and arranged the wood. Then he bound his son Isaac and put him on the altar on top of the wood. Abraham stretched out his hand and seized the knife to kill his son.

But the angel of Yahweh called to him from heaven. "Abraham, Abraham," he said. "I am here," he replied. "Do not raise your hand against the boy," the angel said. "Do not harm him, for now I know that you fear God. You have not refused me your son, your only son." Then looking up, Abraham saw a ram caught by its horns in a bush. Abraham took the ram and offered it as a burnt offering in place of his son. Abraham called this place "Yahweh provides," and hence the saying today, On the mountain Yahweh provides.

The angel of Yahweh called Abraham a second time from heaven. "I swear by my own self—it is Yahweh who speaks—because you have done this, because you have not refused me your son, your only son, I will shower blessings upon you, I will make your descendants as many as the stars of heaven and the grains of sand on the seashore. Your descendants shall gain possession of the gates of their enemies. All the nations of the earth shall bless themselves by your descendants, as a reward for your obedience."

Abraham went back to his servants, and together they set out for Beersheba, and he settled in Beersheba.

[GENESIS 22:1–19]

Like the story of Jonah, the story of the sacrifice of Isaac is also one of the very great examples of Israelitic narrative skill. The Old Testament scholar

The story of the sacrifice of Isaac is a saga. In the patriarchal sagas, centuries-long religious experiences of the Israelite people are collected and condensed. (*Reproduction of Schnorr von Carolsffeld's "Sacrifice of Isaac," courtesy of Prints Division, New York Public Library, Astor, Lenox and Tilden Foundations.*)

Gerhard von Rad calls it properly "the most profound and perfect in form of all patriarchal narratives."[14]

The material described is monstrous. How easy it would have been, therefore, to depict the psychic state of Abraham or the final conversation between him and his son, in a dramatic way. None of the monstrosity of the event is withheld—and yet, the narrative is so restrained! It is packed with dramatic tension—but this is not on the surface but is concealed in the almost sober enumeration of events.

Of course one must read carefully a passage such as the one in which Abraham is described as giving Isaac the wood to carry for the burnt offering, while he himself takes knife and fire, lest his child suffer an injury. Or the passage which describes how father and son have arrived at their destination, and the narrative becomes suddenly more and more exact and precise:

> When they arrived at the place God had pointed out to him, Abraham built an altar there, and arranged the wood. Then he bound his son Isaac and put him on the altar on top of the wood. Abraham stretched out his hand and seized the knife to kill his son.
>
> [GENESIS 22:9–10]

The narrative becomes slower and more hesitant. Not a word is said about Abraham's emotional state, but with this simple concatenation of verbs all is said that need be. The entire later biblical art of narrative springs from the patriarchal stories in Genesis, among which the story of the sacrifice of Isaac is the most beautiful and the most moving.

In what does the difference between the narrative of the sacrifice of Isaac and the narrative of Jonah consist? Must both tales be assigned to the same genre, or are these two different genres? Let us examine them closely.

In the Book of Jonah it became clear, especially in the last scene, that the narrative serves didactic purposes. The drama involving the castor-oil plant, the worm, and the hot wind is produced only so that the great suffering of God may be juxtaposed to the small suffering of Jonah. The reader is dismissed with a question, which he must answer himself.

All of this is completely absent from the story of the sacrifice of Isaac. Here the tale ends not with a question but with a final remark which rounds things off.

> Abraham went back to his servants, and together they set out for Beersheba, and he settled in Beersheba.
>
> [GENESIS 22:19]

The tale is thus intended to report an event from Abraham's life. It is intended to provide *history*. Whether "history" is to be understood in this context as we understand it today, will concern us very closely. For the time being let us simply hold fast to the realization that the tale of the sacrifice of Isaac is intended to provide history. It looks back into the past.

This backward look into the actual past becomes even clearer in the note which closes the first part of the story, namely that Abraham called the place "Yahweh provides" and that it is still called so today. So even in ancient times in Israel there was a connection between our narrative and a specific place. When the tale was told, the listener was reminded of the place, and, in reverse, the story of the sacrifice of Isaac was probably handed down and retold in this very spot. Whatever the apparent relationship of place and tale, the tale of the sacrifice of Isaac is ancient tradition consciously followed. This is shown by the explanation of the name *Yahweh provides*.

With this we have already arrived at a further difference from the Book of Jonah. The Book of Jonah is relatively recent. As we saw, it looks back on Nineveh and the Assyrian Empire as a grandeur of the past. It may have originated and at once been written down between 400 and 200 B.C. Many motifs and themes of the Book of Jonah may be older. But the tale as a whole is a literary composition. It is by no means the final stage of a traditional story first orally transmitted.

In the narrative of the sacrifice of Isaac we see a difference. It must be very old, and before being committed to writing, it must have been told orally again and again over a long period of time. For this there are sure indications: If one for a moment disregards the introductory expression ("it happened some time later") and the final clause ("[Abraham] settled in Beersheba"), the tale is a rounded unit in itself. It has a clear arrangement in the beginning and a genuine conclusion at the end. Narrative tension is generated, achieves its climax, and is released. That is one side. On the other side, Abraham and Isaac in the tale both are presumed to be familiar figures. When both of these factors are taken into account, that the tale is a complete unit in itself, and yet belongs in a larger framework—that is, in a milieu where much is told about Abraham and his family—it is clear that we have here a real *narrative*, at first orally transmitted.

A further difference from the Book of Jonah: There the tale is told about one individual. We saw that the readers of Jonah were supposed to recognize themselves in the figure of Jonah, and that in Jonah Israel has a mirror held up to it; but the narrative, when all is said and done, is about one person. His family is not mentioned. His past and his future are not of interest.

Quite a different situation obtains in the narrative of the sacrifice of Isaac. Here the listener learns a piece of family history; even more, he learns a piece of the history of Israel. For what happens to Abraham and Isaac is history of the founders of the race and thus history of the whole people.

Above all, the tale actually derives its life from the tension between past and future. The hearers know Abraham's past; that he had no heir, that he received God's promise of an heir, and that Isaac is this heir. And now Isaac is to be sacrificed.

For Jewish hearers this is something much more frightful than the sacrifice of a child. It is the loss of the future, the withdrawal of the promise, and, with that, final abandonment on the part of God. In the moment when God releases him from sacrificing his son, the promise and the future are accorded to Abraham anew. The angel of God speaks also in a very detailed and consistent way about this when he calls a second time from

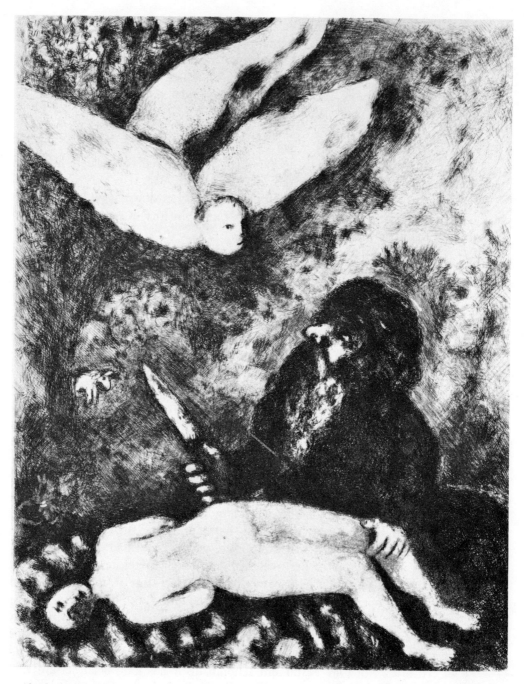

Abraham is a historical figure. He is, however, at the same time a great artistic condensation of what Israel experienced over hundreds of years. ("*Abraham Ready to Sacrifice His Son*," *Marc Chagall,* © A.D.A.G.P., *Paris, 1978; courtesy of the Brooklyn Museum.*)

heaven. The promise from the lips of the angel, moreover, demonstrates very clearly that Abraham is the key to Israel's destiny:

> ". . . because you have done this, because you have not refused me your son, your only son, I will shower blessings upon you, I will make your descendants as many as the stars of heaven. . . ."
>
> [GENESIS 22:16–17]

Let us summarize: (1) The narrative of the sacrifice of Isaac is intended not only to teach but also to provide real history. (2) It is very old. It was orally transmitted a long time before being written down. (3) Its intention is to narrate, in a portion of Abraham's family history, a portion of the history of the people of Israel.

This should make plain that this is quite a different genre from that of the instructive narrative, as illustrated by the Book of Jonah. This is real history. Events from the past are to be narrated.

On the other hand, this history is not exactly like our modern concept of history. Even the fact that the history of an entire people is presented as the family history of the tribal ancestor shows the difference. To condense in such a way the confused, complex destinies of many individuals into the destiny of one single man would be forbidden to contemporary historical writing.

Also the fact that here the history of a man and of a people are conceived and presented almost exclusively as *history with God* constitutes a profound difference from contemporary historical writing. When modern man attempts to understand history, he confines himself consistently to purely secular cause and effect. God does not appear in the modern presentation of history; and certainly not God's promises either. In the narrative of the sacrifice of Isaac, on the other hand, the content is the *promise*, the promise given by God, which he seems to withdraw and then present anew.

All this is, to be sure, real experience, which Israel had to undergo ever and again in the course of her existence and which therefore could be firmly asserted in the narrative of the sacrifice of Isaac. But it is experience of faith, which is open only to those who really believe.

A further difference from contemporary historical writing is this: The historical experiences written down in the narrative of the sacrifice of Isaac were not made all at once, at one single point in Israel's history, but extend over centuries. For Old Testament scholarship it has long been certain that the religious-historical roots of our tale reach deep down into Palestine's past. For the custom of sacrificing the first-born to God, as one's most precious possession, in times of need or on other special occasions is extremely ancient. Often such a sacrifice was made within the framework of a vow. From a certain time it must have been possible, then, in a vow of this kind to *substitute* a sacrificial animal for the child. The substitution was probably carried out in a few specially reserved sanctuaries. It is clear that between a time in which children were slaughtered, as the most costly sacrifice to God, and a later time when such victims were replaced by animals, a quite specific religious experience, a deeper knowledge of God, must have taken place. God does not desire human sacrifices: He wants the human heart; he wants faith and trust. Experiences of this kind have formed our history.

On the other hand experiences have been recorded in this story which come from a much later time—for example, the experience that God blessed Israel, that he made it great, and that he gave it the land it longed for. All this is announced in the angel's second speech—and this speech is plainly a late accretion to the tale. This is seen by the very fact that the angel of Yahweh appears a second time. Originally the tale of the sacrifice of Isaac ended with the sentence "Abraham called this place 'Yahweh provides.'"

These of course are not all the historical experiences revealed behind the various layers of our tale. We have already seen that behind the tale stands the experience of God giving his promise, seeming to withdraw it, and then restoring it. All this and much more concrete, constantly renewed experience is woven into the tale of the sacrifice of Isaac and, what is more, at quite different times.

To which genre then should we assign a text which undertakes to narrate the history of a people, but by way of the history of an individual and his family; which reflects the manifold experiences of a whole people over long periods of time, which, finally, before it was transmitted to writing, was handed down orally for centuries? For a text of this kind only one designation is fitting: *saga!*

If the concept of saga finds ever more application in modern biblical scholarship, it has by no means the negative connotation familiar to many contemporaries—namely, a fantastic tale from long ago, more or less invented. Saga in the literary, critical sense means, rather simply, a tale which has been orally transmitted for a long time and in which the experiences of the community, the lore and self-understanding of previous generations have been preserved.

Almost all the patriarchal narratives of Genesis and many other stories of the Old Testament are sagas in this sense. Their truth is not simply that of external fact, to be sure, nor simply an inward truth as in the Book of Jonah. Behind the patriarchal narratives there stands the real experience of history, which, indeed, does not obviously coincide with the external course of the tale. Abraham, Isaac, and Jacob are historical figures. But at the same time they are great artistic condensations of Israel's experience over the centuries—namely, that she was called and guided by God, that despite all human failure God stands by his promises, that he can lead his people into darkness, but that in the end he changes all suffering into blessing. Israel has incorporated this faith, from manifold, extensive experiences, into its understanding of itself; it has pictured that faith in a personal way and made it comprehensible and visible through the patriarchal sagas.[15]

Reflection about the various forms of human discourse brings us today to the realization that the saga is the adequate and perhaps the only form whereby the experiences of the kind described, made by an entire people, can be consigned to language. The concept of saga, therefore, for the contemporary biblical scholar, is not a negative but a positive one.

—— 5 ——

The Rebellion of Absalom

The foregoing reflections concerning similitude, instructive narrative, and saga must not lead us into assuming that there is no historical writing at all in the Bible. That would be quite wrong. Thus, for example, the *succession history* of David (2 SAMUEL 9–20; 1 KINGS 1–2), centuries before Herodotus, the father of Western historical writing, offers us a protracted description of current history with very exact and detailed information. It must be hailed as an unsurpassed masterpeice of ancient oriental historical writing. Of course, this history of the succession to David's throne is no longer extant in its original outline, for it was later worked into the so-called Deuteronomic history, which includes the books of Deuteronomy, Joshua, Judges, 1 and 2 Samuel, and 1 and 2 Kings. Let us select from this history a passage that tells how Absalom, the son of David, organized a rebellion against his own father which brought David into one of the most dangerous situations of his entire reign.

> After this, Absalom procured a chariot and horses, with fifty men to run ahead of him. He would rise early and stand beside the road leading to the gate; and whenever a man with some lawsuit had to come before the king's court, Absalom would call out to him and ask, "What town are you from?" He would answer, "Your servant is from one of the tribes in Israel." Then Absalom would say, "Look, your case is sound and just, but there is not one deputy of the king's who will listen to

you." Absalom would go on to say, "Oh, who will appoint me judge in the land? Then anyone with a lawsuit or a plea could come to me and I would see he had justice." And whenever anyone came up to do homage to him, he would stretch out his hand and take him and kiss him. Absalom acted in this way with all the Israelites who came to the king for justice, and so Absalom seduced the hearts of the men of Israel.

At the end of four years Absalom said to the king, "Allow me to go to Hebron to fulfill the vow I made to Yahweh; for when I was at Geshur in Aram, your servant made this vow: 'If Yahweh brings me back to Jerusalem,' I said, 'I will offer worship to Yahweh in Hebron.'" The king said to him, "Go in peace," so he set off and went to Hebron.

Absalom sent couriers throughout the tribes of Israel, saying, "When you hear the trumpet sound you are to say, 'Absalom is king at Hebron!'" With Absalom there went two hundred men from Jerusalem; they were invited guests and came in all innocence, quite unaware. Absalom sent for Ahitophel the Gilonite, David's counselor, from Giloh his town, and had him with him while he was offering the sacrifices. The conspiracy grew in strength and Absalom's supporters grew in number.

A messenger came to tell David, "The hearts of the men of Israel are now with Absalom." So David said to all his officers who were with him in Jerusalem, "Let us be off, let us fly, or we never shall escape from Absalom. Leave as quickly as you can, in case he mounts a surprise attack and worsts us and puts the city to the sword." The king's officers answered, "Whatever my lord and king decides, we are at your service." The king left on foot with all his household, leaving ten concubines to look after the palace. The king left on foot with all the people and stopped at the last house. All his officers stood at his side. All the Cherethites and all the Pelethites, with Ittai and all the six hundred Gittites who had come in his retinue from Gath, marched past the king. The king said to Ittai the Gittite, "You, why are you coming with us? Go back and stay with the king, for you are a foreigner, an exile too from your homeland. You came only yesterday; should I take you wandering today with us, when I do not know myself where I am going? Go back, take your fellow countrymen with you, and may Yahweh show you kindness and faithfulness." But Ittai answered the king, "As Yahweh lives, and as my lord the king lives, wherever my lord the king may be, for death or life, there will your servant be too." So David said to Ittai, "Go then, and pass on." And Ittai of Gath passed on with all his men and retinue. All the people wept aloud. The king took his stand in the wadi Kidron, and all the people marched past him towards the wilderness."

[2 SAMUEL 15:1–23]

In what does the difference between this narrative and the narrative of the sacrifice of Isaac consist? First we have to say that the story of the sacrifice of Isaac is a tale easily grasped, rounded off, and a closed unit in itself. It has a clear climax; its action, despite all the concealed meaning, is simple and straightforward: God has issued his command, Abraham obeys, and nothing hinders him, God takes back his command.

In the text from the "Succession to David" all this is quite different. The tale is much more spacious. It has already previously told a lot about David and Absalom, and afterwards it flows on like a great stream. But not only is the mass of material much larger; the subject matter is much more complicated and unwieldy.

This can be very well seen in the number of persons who appear. In the story of the sacrifice of Isaac we encounter Abraham, Isaac, two servants, and the angel of Yahweh, who actually stands for God himself. The servants are entirely colorless; even Isaac is somehow relegated to the side; the actual supporters of the action are God and Abraham. The story takes place between them.

In this text on the other hand David and Absalom confront each other as two human actors of equal importance in the plot. But besides them we encounter also a man like Achitophel from Giloh, one of David's cleverest advisors, who switches to the side of the rebels and thereby—as the continuation of the story shows—becomes most dangerous for David. But this is not enough! In our text there are other groupings: the Israelites whose heart Absalom has seduced—an anonymous and invisible but still important factor of history; then the two hundred aristocrats from Jerusalem who have gone with Absalom to Hebron and then have mostly switched to the rebel's side; finally the troops at David's disposal at the moment of revolt, the Cherethites and Pelethites (the royal bodyguard) and the not unwelcome band of the foreigner Ittai. All these persons and groups are by no means only accessories and background but are woven into the events, which are more complicated and intricate and much less perspicuous than in the story of the sacrifice of Isaac.

When we said that the tale of the succession to the throne was much more spacious, this is to be understood finally also in the sense that here in general for the first time a social and political horizon comes into view. Even the first sentences of our text, in which light is cast upon the juridical and administrative practice of David (not exactly to his advantage), make clear that now history—in a much more detailed way than in the sagas of the patriarchs—is seen as the result of manifold political and social entanglements.

A further difference from the story of the sacrifice of Isaac: In our text there is a multitude of concrete details, which indeed function on the level of the narrative but which, from the point of view of the subject matter, or the events, are "accidental." Let us clarify our meaning by an example: In the story of Isaac, when a donkey, wood, fire for the altar of burnt offering, a knife, and finally a ram are encountered, these are the logical and more or less necessary prerequisites of the tale from the point of view of the subject matter.

But when it is reported in our Absalom text that Absalom could induce two hundred men from Jerusalem to go along unsuspecting to Hebron, or that David had at that very time taken up six hundred mercenaries from Gath in the city, or that he left ten concubines behind in his palace, these are concrete details which could just as well have been otherwise. As we have said, these details certainly have their function within the narrative: That two hundred men go along to Hebron without suspecting anything shows how elaborately Absalom set the conspiracy in motion; the episode with the Gittites illumines true loyalty in contrast to the faithlessness of Absalom; and the ten concubines are later confiscated and ravished by Absalom. But all this could naturally have been different in reality from the way it was in the narrative.

The observation that Absalom had acquired a team of horses reveals the character of David's son with economy and precision: Teams of horses were at that time in Israel a new and unheard-of luxury. (*Photo by Friedhelm Heyde, KBW, Stuttgart.*)

A further difference: We have seen how in the saga and even more in the instructive narrative, use is made of typification. The figure of Abraham is, of course, historical, but at the same time the condensation of centuries of faith-experiences of Israel. Jonah is a man in whom stubborn Israel, constantly preoccupied with itself and fleeing from God, is supposed to recognize itself. Nineveh is the symbol of the great, strange, mysterious power of the pagan peoples.

In the Absalom text such use of types does not occur at all. To be sure, David too late became a type. But in our tale he has certainly not yet done so. He and all other figures of the story of the succession to the throne are presented as sharply delineated, unmistakable characters; what is more, with a psychological clarity and exactness by which one can only be astonished. What a light falls on Absalom alone in our relatively brief text: He contrives to obtain a team of horses—at the time an unheard of novelty and an attention-getting luxury; he causes fifty runners to precede him whenever he makes a public appearance; he toadies to the populace; he exploits cleverly the weaknesses of David's administration and juridical practice; he finally waits four years, with uncanny patience and dissimulation, until he can strike at last. In a similar way he had waited for two years, with ice-cold calculation, before murdering his brother Amnon. Up to this time in oriental literature human beings had never been portrayed in such sharp focus.

To this concreteness of character portrayal, the concreteness of place description corresponds. The scene of action of the tale constantly shifts, and is always carefully located: Jerusalem, Hebron, Jerusalem again, the last house at the edge of the city, the wadi of Kidron, the march in the direction of the desert. Let us select Hebron from these geographical indications. Inasmuch as this is the city named as the starting point for the insurrection, a whole background is suggested. It is the city of Absalom's birth—so the inhabitants were probably on his side. It is also the old residence of David, which he had then given up in favor of Jerusalem—very probably a reason for the population of Hebron to be disinclined toward David. For other reasons Hebron was well suited as a starting point for the insurrection: The distance from Jerusalem was not very great; David actually had to leave the capital in great flurry and haste. Also, Hebron was celebrated as a cult center and place of pilgrimage—the pretext of a sacrifice in Hebron seemed to be valid. This entire contemporary historical background is suggested by the mere mention of Hebron. What a difference from the mention of Nineveh in the Book of Jonah or the mention of the cult place in the saga of the sacrifice of Isaac.

Let us come to a final difference. In the story of the sacrifice of Isaac the angel of Yahweh calls down from heaven at the decisive moment and thus turns events around. But already, at the very beginning, the text reads:

"Take your son," God said, "your only son Isaac, whom you love, and go to the land of Moriah. There you shall offer him as a burnt offering on a mountain I will point out to you."

[GENESIS 22:2]

God thus speaks with people; he gives them orders and promises; he interferes decisively and wonderfully in what takes place on earth.

In the succession history of David it would be unthinkable that God should call from heaven. Nor does he perform miracles to change the course of history by their aid. Everything that happens is considered first as internal links of cause and effect. We have already seen how carefully the most varied persons, groups of persons, and social constellations are brought into the picture. This is a decided change from the patriarchal sagas! Here history is now really understood as *secular* history, and therewith the premise for historical writing is given us for the very first time.

It must of course not be overlooked that even in this form of biblical historical writing all events remain open to the action of God. Even the history is now really understood as *secular* history, and therewith the premise directed by God. In our text it does not become apparent. But in other passages, before and after, the narrator sometimes makes a little side comment plainly showing that for him too God is behind everything that happens. Thus in 2 Samuel 11:27, for example, after David's sin against Uriah, we find the apparently inconsequential sentence: "But what David had done displeased Yahweh." The reader here has an inkling that David will not go unpunished for what he has done to Uriah. Thus it is clear that in Israel there is no *purely* secular writing of history. God always remains operative in history and embraces all that has happened. Nevertheless, the difference from the patriarchal sagas is evident: History is taken seriously, and presented as secular history. And that is our concern here.

If we now look back once more, we may say that in the succession history of David we have a form of narrative which we may correctly designate as *historical*. We can no longer speak of saga. This is real history, created with its structure of individuals, groups, and social forces, with its "unlogic" and its accidents. And this creation has constituted a new form: the *historical narrative*.

By the term "historical narrative" we do not mean, of course, that this form of historical presentation was originally, like the legend, orally transmitted—that is, *told*. In the case of the story of the succession to the throne we can say with assurance that its immediate provenance was literary. Its creator must have been an educated man of Solomon's court (ca. 970–30 B.C.), who was probably himself an eyewitness and who also had at his disposal material from archives and much oral information. Its actual setting is most likely a circle of court officials and scholars. The court had a particular interest in the history of the young kingdom, and was also interested in collecting and recording older traditions. Much even speaks for the absolute political motivation of the story: It was intended to give authenticity to Solomon as David's successor. In any case it was a literary work from the beginning.

When, however, we speak of historical narrative, there is another factor. A historical presentation can, after all, treat the events of which it speaks much more abstractly. It can marshal and connect facts from an objective distance; it can insert statements and reflections of the author into the sequence of events. Then we no longer have pure narrative; rather the presentation approaches the nature of a *treatise*. Let us read, bearing this in mind, the following text. It too concerns a political insurrection, namely the conspiracy of Catiline against the Roman state. It is, of course, about nine hundred years more recent than the description of Absalom's revolt. It was written by the Roman historian Sallust (86–34 B.C.), and is the seventeenth chapter of his work *The Conspiracy of Catiline*.

Thus about the first of June in the year when Lucius Caesar and Gaius Figulus were consuls [64 B.C.], he first invited individuals to join him, some by persuasion, others by promises of power; he said that a conspiracy was likely to prove a good investment since the state was so unprepared. When he had scouted out to his satisfaction everything he wanted to know, he called them all together—whoever was motivated by the greatest need and the most flagrant daring. Of the senatorial order there were assembled Publius Lentulus Sura, Publius Autronius, Lucius Cassius Longinus, Gaius Cethegus, Publius and Servius Sulla, the sons of Servius, Lucius Vargunteius, Quintus Annius, Marcus Porcius Laeta, Lucius Bestia, Quintus Curias; further, from the equestrian order there came Marcus Fulvius Nobilius, Lucius Stabilius, Publius Gabinius Capito, Gaius Cornelius; in addition many from the colonies and towns joined who at home passed for noblemen. Also there were several noble participants of youthful status involved less openly, who were induced to join rather by hope of future leadership than by any need or other pressing reason. But most young men, especially of noble birth, were favorably inclined to Catiline's undertaking. They had opportunity, in their leisure, to live either on a luxurious scale or moderately, but they preferred uncertainty to certainty, and war to peace. Some there were at the time who believed that Marcus Licinius Crassus was aware of Catiline's project, because Gnaeus Pompey, who was hostile to him, was commanding a large army. Crassus would have wished anyone's resources to be lined up with favorable balance of power against Pompey, confident also that if Catiline's conspiracy should prevail, he would easily be the foremost among the victors.[16]

Of course this text too is not a pure treatise. It too tells a story. But how differently than in our passage about Absalom! With what art and thoughtfulness is the thread of the action broken again and again by judgments and reflections of the author! Directly after the text here cited comes a long passage about an earlier conspiracy in which Catiline was also involved. And elsewhere there are passages which provide pages upon pages of Sallust's personal reflections.

In contrast to this the Absalom story is *pure* narrative. It offers history by way of stories. And thus it is everywhere in the Bible, even where biblical historical writing, as here, reaches its highest level. Always a living, moving story is told, and always the narrator conceals himself completely behind his narrative. This of course has both advantages and disadvantages.

The disadvantages: Pure narrative must always stylize reality. It must leave a lot out. It must simplify a lot. It only indirectly permits a judgment on the part of the author. It gives no accounting for its sources and authorities.

But its inestimable advantages are these: color, life, drama, vividness. It can stir emotions and stimulate reflectiveness. Above all, it is not easily forgotten. For what it says it says with an intensity and depth from which the pure treatise is excluded.

— 6 —

Court Chronicle and Travel Journal

In the passage from the *Conspiracy of Catiline* cited above, a long series of personal names is listed: "Of the senatorial order there were assembled . . ." etc. This enumeration is set off clearly, with its simple catalogue of names, from the rest of the passage. Such enumerations are called *lists*, and are rightly considered a proper literary genre. In our case the list of Catiline's conspirators is perfectly integrated into the rest of the passage, and it is quite possible that Sallust was the first to compile it. Therefore it would never have existed for itself alone.

But there are also lists which exist as isolated, self-contained forms. Let us think of files of persons and objects, telephone books or address books, indexes or inventories. They all agree—as far as form is concerned—that in

EXT.	NAME	DIV/DEPT	LOC.

EXT.	NAME	DIV/DEPT	LOC.
4718	Galante, Joan	PER/028	3
4710	Galway, Diane	PER/028	3
4704	Galway, Robert	PER/028	3
4678	Garnier, Claire	FIN/004	1
4043	Garramone, Anthony	BCL/045	1
4657	Geier, June	PER/025	3
4044	Genis, Chris	BCL/045	1
4864	Gennings, Carol	FIN/049	1
4127	Gentilcore, Joan	PUB/185	3
4482	George, Beverly	FIN/012	1
4331	George, George	BCL/042	3
4306	Gerlach, Edward	BCL/042	3
4500	Gernon, Winifred	FIN/014	1
4828	Giossi, Lydia	FIN/049	1
4387	Gitsas, Nicholas	MAN/057	3
4813	Glanze, Vion	FIN/049	1
4695	Glass, Virginia	FIN/002	1
4712	Godfrey, Thomas	MAN/035	6
4602	Godoy, Lilyan	FIN/023	3
4742	Goetchius, Jo-Ann	PUB/197	3
4673	Gomes, Alice - Cashier	FIN/079	1
4473	Goodrick, Charlotte	FIN/018	1
4655	Goold, Katherine	PER/025	3

Telephone directories belong to the genre *list*. In a list, words of some given kind are set one after the other.

each of them words of a specific kind are put together; that is the characteristic feature of a list.

The genre *list* is not only widespread but also very old. We encounter it in the oldest written documents of mankind. There are lists of kings, of conquered cities and provinces, of warriors and officials, or of consecrated gifts for shrines.

Of course we find lists in the Bible, which is so extremely rich in fixed forms. Especially in the Old Testament there are numerous instances. Let the list of the senior officers and officials of David serve as an example:

> Joab commanded the whole army; Benaiah son of Jehoiada commanded the Cherethites and Pelethites; Adoram was in charge of forced labor; Jehoshaphat son of Ahilud was recorder; Sheva, secretary; Zadok and Abiathar, priests. Ira the Jairite was also a priest of David.
>
> [2 SAMUEL 20:23–26]

This list of officials is in any case very old. It comes from the time of David or Solomon. And probably it first existed independently. Not until centuries later did the author of the Deuteronomic history incorporate it into his presentation. The list which begins the thirteenth chapter of Acts is a similar case. Here, to be sure, we are not dealing with a list of officials but are concerned with a list of the leading members of the congregation of Antioch in the time of Paul:

> In the church at Antioch the following were prophets and teachers: Barnabas, Simeon called Niger, and Lucius of Cyrene, Manean, who had been brought up with Herod the tetrarch, and Saul.
>
> [ACTS 13:1]

Pharaoh Ramses II had lists of the places he had conquered carved into the pedestal of a colossal statue of himself in Luxor. (*Photo by Luc H. Grollenberg, Nijmegen.*)

This list too is older than the work in which it is found. The writer of the Acts of the Apostles has already taken it over and built it into his historical work in an appropriate place.

It is clear, of course, that such old, original lists as these must represent a true treasure-trove for the historian. They offer much more than just a few names. Behind the names, carefully handed down, an entire historical background opens out. Thus the list preserved in 2 Samuel 20 permits valuable insights into David's administrative practice. And Acts 13:1 shows us in outline the structure of the primitive Church in Antioch: As yet there was no institutional arrangement with a bishop at the head of the congregation and a council of presbyters and deacons, but the congregation was led by prophets and teachers—in other words, by charismatics.

Closely akin to the genre of the list is the *chronicle*. For in a certain sense it too is an index. Not, to be sure, an index of things and persons but an index of events, which are set down in the most concise possible way, usually in regular intervals of time. If such data are recorded every day, we speak of a journal; if every year, we speak of *annals* (Latin *annus*=year).

The genre of the chronicle is also very old. At the ancient oriental royal courts it must have proven practical at some time to compile important events of a year in a reign, or of the entire period of a given monarch's rule, and to preserve this chronicle in the government archives with lists and documents. In addition the great sanctuaries, which were also state institutions, had their own chronicles and their own temple archives.

Of course there were such official chronicles in the time of David and his successors. The names of three chronicles of the monarchy have been handed down to us in the Old Testament. There was a "Book of the Events of Solomon's Reign," a court chronicle obviously; a "Book of the Events of the Days of the Kings of Israel," a court chronicle of the northern kingdom; and a "Book of the Events of the Days of the Kings of Judah," a chronicle of the southern kingdom. Unfortunately none of these chronicles has been preserved. But the author of the Deuteronomic history has built parts of them into his presentation of history, or at least taken them over in selections. We will quote one of the selections from "The Chronicle of the Kings of Israel." It is about Elah, who was king of the northern kingdom from 886 to 885.

In the twenty-sixth year of Asa King of Judah, Elah son of Baasha became king of Israel at Tirzah, for two years. Zimri, one of his officers, captain of half his chariotry, plotted against him. While he was at Tirzah, drinking himself senseless in the house of Arza who was master of the palace in Tirzah, Zimri came in, struck him down and killed him in the twenty-seventh year of Asa king of Judah, and succeeded him. On his accession, as soon as he was seated on the throne, he butchered

Baasha's entire family, not leaving him a single male, or any relations or friends. *Zimri destroyed the whole House of Baasha, in accordance with the word which Yahweh had spoken through the prophet Jehu, because of all the sins of Baasha and his son Elah into which they had led Israel, provoking the anger of Yahweh, the God of Israel, with their useless idols.*

The history of Elah, his entire career, is not all this recorded in the Book of the Annals of the Kings of Israel?

[1 KINGS 16:8–14]

Everyone who reads this text immediately notices that this is a unique genre. It is certainly not a narrative. Dates and facts from a long period of time are simply listed together. First the year of the commencement of Elah's reign, indicated with the help of the chronology of the contemporaneously reigning king in the southern kingdom; then the name of the king; then the name of his father; then the place of his residence; and then the extent of time of his reign. Sentences follow about the overthrow of the king by his soldiers. But even there there is no narrative, just a concisely styled report. In this form this could certainly have been included in "The Chronicle of the Kings of Israel." Then, however, come two sentences (which we have italicized) which show quite a different structure. They no longer simply report but give a theological interpretation of what has already been reported: that the king and his family suffered so dreadfully was God's punishment for the worship of idols by Elah and his father. Yahweh had threatened this punishment beforehand through the prophet Jehu. Thus now the soberly listed data concerning Elah's reign are set into the religious area of tension of guilt and punishment. Secular history is opened in the direction of God and made transparent. This theological illumination of bare historical facts certainly had not yet taken place in the royal court chronicle. It was first added to his source by the writer of the Deuteronomic history. Finally, in the last sentence the writer expressly names his source and emphasizes the fact that there is more to find in it about King Elah:

The history of Elah, his entire career, is not all this recorded in the Book of the Annals of the Kings of Israel?

[1 KINGS 16:14]

In the Old Testament there are a great number of such texts, in which dates and events are listed in most concise form and which must be assigned to the genre of the chronicle. Does this exist also in the New Testament?

The answer is simple and at the same time most informative. At least in the Gospels there is not a single text of the kind. Apparently the New Testament communities had not the slightest interest in starting a chronicle

From the scribal schools of the temple and the royal court new literary categories and forms were forthcoming: *list, chronicle, wisdom book*. Here a royal scribe of the fifth dynasty in Egypt is seen. The officials of Solomon would have looked like this as they engaged in their work. (*Photo courtesy of Service de Documentation photographique de la Réunion des Musées Nationaux, Paris, France.*)

of Jesus' life. The reason is obvious. We have seen that the chronicle has a very definite actual setting: the schools of the scribes and archives of the royal court or of the central sanctuaries. The genre presupposes institutions that already have a long history behind them and that plan on a long future.

No such thing was the case among the early Christian communities. They possessed no official archives. They had no sanctuaries, and above all no central sanctuary. Nor did they have an official past. Their past was at most the proclamation and salvific work of Jesus. But this was, strictly speaking, not a past but a living present in word and sacrament. Nor did they anticipate an earthly future, but lived in expectation of the imminent second coming of Jesus Christ. Communities who live and believe these things need neither archive nor chronicle. Thus we must not be surprised that the genre of the official chronicle does not exist in primitive Christian communities chiefly concerned with Jesus Christ.

In the New Testament we encounter only a private chronicle. But this also does not have the life of Jesus as its subject matter but specific portions of Paul's missionary journeys. It is written in the latter part of Acts. We will quote an especially typical passage. It begins with the departure of Paul and his companions from Miletus. Just before, a meeting with the presbyters of the Ephesus community had been described.

> When we had at last torn ourselves away from them and put to sea, we set a straight course and arrived at Cos; the next day we reached Rhodes, and from there went straight on to Patara. Here we found a ship bound for Phoenicia, so we went on board and sailed in her. After sighting Cyprus and leaving it to port, we sailed to Syria and put in at Tyre, since the ship was to unload her cargo there. We sought out the disciples and stayed there a week. Speaking in the Spirit, they kept telling Paul not to go on to Jerusalem, but when our time was up we set off. Together with the women and children they all escorted us on our way till we were out of the town. When we reached the beach, we knelt down and prayed; then, after saying good-bye to each other, we went aboard and they returned home. The end of our voyage came when we landed at Ptolemais, where we greeted the brothers and stayed one day with them. The next day we left and came to Caesarea. Here we called on Philip the Evangelist, one of the Seven, and stayed with him. He had four virgin daughters who were prophets. When we had been there several days . . ."
>
> [ACTS 21:1–10]

This text too is by no means a narrative. Rather, just as in the chronicle of 1 Kings 16, it is a listing of dates and facts in the most concise form. But here the internal pattern of articulation is not the period of a year but instead a day-by-day pattern. The style is that of a travel journal rewritten after the journey, into which from time to time (not every day) concise entries are made in order to hold fast important details of a rather long journey. In a journal of this kind one notes the stopping-places and details of the route; the time needed for each specific distance is carefully recorded; the names of one's hosts are written down; one also notes the quality of the hospitality one has received; finally a record is made of unusual events which should not be forgotten.

Most of this is found here in our text. The stopping-places are named: Cos, Rhodes, Patara, Tyre, Ptolemais, and Caesarea. Furthermore the details of the route are included: they sailed directly to Cos, leaving Cyprus to the north. At three points the time required is given more exactly: From Miletus to Cos, from Cos to Rhodes, and from Ptolemais to Caesarea one day each was required. In Tyre the company remained seven days, in Ptolemais one. At Caesarea the names of the hosts are given: the family of Philip the Deacon. In regard to Tyre and Ptolemais it is at least noted that the travelers slept overnight with fellow Christians. The emotional farewell in Tyre receives special comment. The only remarkable event recorded is what happened at Tyre: The members of the congregation urgently advised Paul against going to Jerusalem.

Here are a relatively large number of soberly listed facts recorded in the smallest possible space—and that is the distinguishing feature of the chronicle genre. It is also important in determining the genre to note that isolated facts are mentioned without being used as a potential thread of narrative. Thus, when Philip's daughters are mentioned, it is indicated that they had the gift of prophecy. In a narrative one would expect, after such a comment, that one of the daughters or all of them would then actually prophesy. But this does not happen. In similar fashion stopping-places are named where nothing at all happens. A narrative would mention the name of a place only if it were the scene of a real action. This above all shows this passage to be not narrative but enumeration. We do not have a narrative, but a report before us—specifically, a report in the form of a travel journal.

How did this travel journal, which also turns up in other chapters of Acts, come about? Was the writer a contemporary of Paul? Did he go with him on some of his travels, note the most important events, and incorporate part of his notes into the structure of Acts? For a long time this was the opinion of New Testament scholarship.

In the course of time, however, it has been recognized how difficult this assumption is. For—to name the chief difficulty at once—we know very well from Paul's letters what Paul's theology was like. The picture of Pauline theology drawn in Acts, however, deviates so much from this that the book can hardly be by a companion of Paul. It already looks back on Paul as a great missionary of the past. If modern exegesis is correct in this statement, then the sections of Acts which are in the form of a travel journal cannot be from the writer of the book himself and at the same time the journal of one of Paul's actual companions. Therefore it has been recently assumed that the writer of Acts possessed a travel journal which was once written down by a real companion of Paul. He carefully evaluated it, then took from it verbatim certain portions.

But this assumption also creates considerable difficulties. One would necessarily expect the form of the travel journal to extend continuously over major parts of the second section of Acts. But this is not so. Only smaller passages really present the strict form of a report. Above all, however, there are important omissions in some places regarding the travels and missionary work of St. Paul; these could hardly be explained in the case of a continuous travel journal available to the writer.

To avoid these difficulties, in very recent times a path to a third solution has been opened. If the Acts is by a Christian of postapostolic times, no longer acquainted with Paul, we must assume that he gathered (after the fact) reports from still living companions of Paul about the missionary journeys, whether the reports were oral or written. In this process a mass of material could have been collected, no doubt of varied authenticity and unevenly distributed as far as chronology goes. The writer of Acts then gave his material the form of a travel journal where he had available many single points of information, including even perhaps reports of eyewitnesses. In this way single bits of information could best be put into a whole; in this way also the reader could get an idea of what had happened from authoritative sources who had seen in person some of the events described.

We need not here decide which of these three solutions is the correct or more probable one. However the form of a travel journal originated in Acts, no historian can disregard the point that the book offers an abundance of very valuable information in these very portions.

—— 7 ——

The Arrest of Jesus

In the previous section genres were treated which enumerate and report: list, chronicle, travel journal. It became plain that these genres are of special value to the historian. Thus the question emerges: Why does the Bible not actually give much more extensive reports in this form? Why, for example, does the New Testament offer us no chronicle of Jesus' life, no clear chronology of his public appearances, no list of the places where he

The presentation of the arrest of Jesus in Mark gives us a long list of historical details. Nonetheless the account is more than a report. It tries at the same time to clarify the event from the standpoint of faith. (*Reproduction of Gustave Doré's "The Kiss of Judas" courtesy of Prints Division, the New York Public Library, Astor, Lenox and Tilden Foundations.*)

preached? And, above all, why does the New Testament offer no exact reports about the events themselves? Why did it show so little interest in these things? We have already received a partial answer: The primitive Church was not interested in chronicle and report because it had no expectations of a long future and therefore no concern about objectification of the past. This is a correct but insufficient answer. We must amplify it in what follows. Our concrete example will be Mark's account of the arrest of Jesus.

Even while he was still speaking, Judas, one of the Twelve, came up with a number of men armed with swords and clubs, sent by the chief priests and the scribes and the elders. Now the traitor had arranged a signal with them. "The one I kiss," he had said, "he is the man. Take him in charge, and see he is well guarded when you lead him away." So when the traitor came, he went straight up to Jesus and said, "Rabbi!" and kissed him. The others seized him and took him in charge. Then one of the bystanders drew his sword and struck out at the high priest's servant, and cut off his ear.

Then Jesus spoke. "Am I a brigand," he said, "that you had to set out to capture me with swords and clubs? I was among you teaching in the Temple day after day and you never laid hands upon me. But this is to fulfill the scriptures." And they all deserted him and ran away. A young man who followed him had nothing on but a linen cloth. They caught hold of him, but he left the cloth in their hands and ran away naked.

[MARK 14:43–52]

How should the form of this passage be judged? First we notice that elements are encountered here which would be very appropriate for a report, that is, for a listing of bare facts. If we enumerate these reportive elements in order, we get a picture like this:

1) Judas suddenly appears and an armed squadron with him.
2) Judas approaches Jesus, greets him with the appellation "Rabbi," and kisses him.
3) The squadron with Judas arrests Jesus.
4) One of the bystanders draws his sword and cuts off the ear of an opponent.
5) Jesus' disciples flee.
6) A young man runs away naked when someone takes hold of his clothing.

All these are soberly formulated facts which could easily constitute a report. Such a report would even reflect what is typical for every really historical event: the disunity and fragmentation of what happens. In reality things never go off smoothly: There are always coincidences, something goes suddenly awry; things happen which only real life can invent. Bearing this in mind, let us re-examine elements 4–6 in the above list, which actually must have taken place at the same time: Jesus' friends and acquaintances escape; only one thinks of counterattack and draws his sword; a young man flees naked. All this reflects the confusion typical of such situations. It is also characteristic that it is not at all certain whether the man who drew his sword was one of the disciples, to say nothing of the fact that his name is not mentioned. It was dark then, and afterward no one knew exactly what had happened.

The episode of the young man who flees away naked fits especially well into this disunity of happening. Despite the gravity of the whole situation, this scene has ridiculous aspects. The other evangelists probably omitted it for that very reason. What had such an episode to do with salvation history? But just such things are the stuff of real history. Life is always a mixture of the sensible and the absurd, the serious and the ridiculous, the important and the trivial. Seen as a whole, the business with the young man is as unimportant as the fact that Paul's ship sailed to the north of Cyprus. But that's how things appear when we want to report them precisely and exactly. The facts basic to our text would thus have been very well suited to record Jesus' arrest in the linguistic form of a report.

We must also note in this connection how little expanded Mark's text is in the sense of Christian legend. Such expansions occur quite soon, even within the Gospel tradition. Soon people will want to know, Who was the man who drew his sword? Answer: One of the apostles, namely Peter (John 18:10). One asks, What was the name of the servant of the high priest whose ear was cut off? Answer: His name was Malchus (John 18:10). And which ear did the poor man lose? Answer: The right ear (Luke 22:50). And was it possible that Jesus would leave a man with such an injury right there where he was? Answer: No, impossible! Jesus healed the wound (Luke 22:51). And finally one wants to know, What did Jesus actually say when he was betrayed by Judas' kiss? He couldn't have just kept silent! Answer: "Jesus said, 'Judas, are you betraying the Son of Man with a kiss?'" (Luke 22:48). These are all later expansions which could have easily been invented. They are not in Mark, and therefore in any case are more recent. From them we see how strictly and practically Mark presents his data and how much closer he is to the actual events. So in this case all the premises were given to make possible a genuine report from the material at hand—with a real listing of data and facts.

Actually, however, this did not happen. The arrest of Jesus is, even in Mark, not a report, any more than in the other evangelists. Rather it is a

The episode of the young man fleeing naked has something ridiculous about it. But precisely that sort of thing, with its chance quality and its incongruity, belongs to true history.

narrative: It attempts to grasp what has happened in depth, to illuminate its background, and to understand it in the light of faith.

Even the sentence "Now the traitor had arranged a signal with them" abandons the standpoint of an eyewitness and attempts to indicate the machinations which had previously been spun in the background. Furthermore, there is clear subjective judgment in the use of the word "traitor." Interpretation and evaluation, moreover, also are inherent in the formula "Judas, one of the Twelve." The reader remembers, when he hears this, everything previously recorded in the Gospel about the Twelve: the common life which Jesus had given them, the promise he had offered them. Now one of these Twelve is betraying him. Jesus' loneliness is implied. Even his friends did not understand him.

Then we have to note how carefully, in the second part of the narrative, the statements are composed: One of those present seizes his weapon. As a counterweight to this helpless and completely senseless behavior comes the calm, sure statement of Jesus to his adversaries. But his words are a signal for flight to his disciples. Up to this moment they had hesitated as it were. But now we read, "They all deserted him and ran away." As an appendix to this, finally, a single episode is described, with which the general flight is to be illuminated and concretized. Thus, at the end of our narrative unit the great desolation of Jesus is made plain; it had been previously intimated. Jesus must go his way alone. It is certainly now clear how carefully the confused, unrelated hodgepodge of facts taken all together is subordinated to the orderly progression of a modified narrative sequence.

But even within the entire passage the construction is recognizable: To Judas' betrayal in the first part the helpless, hapless flight of the disciples at the end corresponds. But in the middle stands the calm, firm word of Jesus: From this word we can read most clearly that our text is more than a report. That the historical Jesus cannot have spoken in just this way at the time of his arrest is obvious. A man who is supposed to be arrested without attracting attention is not allowed to make a speech at the moment of his capture. But above all, Jesus is preaching to the wrong congregation. What he says is directed only to those responsible, the leaders of the people, not the policemen who capture him as they were commanded. Luke noticed this and arranged his narrative in such a way that only high priests, temple officials, and elders are present. (Compare Luke 22:52 with Mark 14:48.) But the difficulty of the wrong audience disappears anyway when one realizes that the sentence referred to is not intended to reproduce exactly the historical words of Jesus but to interpret the event of the arrest for the reader. In this case it is quite meaningful for Jesus to turn to those who motivate his death. In doing so, he even speaks of the fulfilling of scripture. Jesus' words are intended to make clear to the reader how unjust and treacherous his adversaries' procedure was, but also that in the Passion nothing quite senseless or incomprehensible took place, but that scripture was being fulfilled—that is to say, that salvation history was being accomplished.

So our text is certainly not a report. It is rather a historical narrative interpreting the events of the time; it arranges the single facts sensibly and thereby interprets them, but it also does not hesitate to put words on Jesus' lips which illuminate and explain the historical event.

This interconnection of facts and simultaneous interpretation of the facts is characteristic of the whole Passion story, indeed not only of the Passion story but of most of the narrative texts of the Gospels. Of course the mixture of pure information and interpretation is varied. Sometimes one is preponderant, sometimes the other. But never in the Gospels is there mere report, which reproduces things only in their external sequence and dispenses with all interpretation. Why is this? We return to the question we asked already, at the beginning of this chapter.

Why do the Gospels offer us no *report* of specific portions of Jesus' life, for example, concerning his Passion? One should ask, to be consistent, the counterquestion: What would have really been achieved if the primitive Church had reported the course of the Passion in the correct sequence, with many details and no interpretive addition, in the form of a chronicle? Would we know then what really happened? I doubt it.

Let us imagine that the Passion narratives of the Gospels had never been written. Instead, let us suppose that the final hours of Jesus' life had been filmed with a secret camera, and everything that was said had been recorded by a hidden microphone. Sound and picture would have been synchronized, and this film would have been presented to us today, uncut and without commentary. What would we know then?

Well, we would certainly know a mass of details not found in the Gospels. We would know exactly how the arrest of Jesus was managed. We would finally know just what took place before the Sanhedrin. Also we would know what the procedure was at the Crucifixion, and all the external details. All that would be very important, exciting, and shattering. But would we really know, with all this help, what was actually happening that day in Jerusalem and on Golgotha? I assert emphatically: We would know nothing about what was actually happening.

For we would see how a Jew was executed on a cross by Roman soldiers. That would indeed be shattering. And yet, the Roman garrison was going through the same procedure with thousands of Jews. Jesus' death on the cross would then mean very little to us if we did not know why he was tried and why he was executed. But would that really be clear to us from the proceedings? Would exact knowledge of the external course of the proceedings reveal why Jesus was ultimately done away with? Hardly!

To find out something about this really, we would have to know about Jesus' previous life, his actions, his preaching, and his aims. Even here our documentary of the Passion would fail. We would need for this a documentary film about the whole period of Jesus' public activity. But would that really help us? Could we even remotely grasp Jesus' claims without being acquainted with the Old Testament? Can we understand Jesus at all if we do not examine his life bearing in mind that here history, between God and Israel, has entered its last, decisive phase? But how should these dimensions of history become plain through mere documentation, through bare reporting of an external sequence of events? Here mere report fails; here the chronicle, with its marshaling of facts, fails as well. The deeper dimension of history, its secret and its internal meaning, can be made visible only by exegesis and interpretation.

With this we have come to the most profound reason why the genres of report and chronicle could not suffice for the primitive Church. The Church was concerned after all with the salvation-historical meaning of the event on Golgotha, and with the interpretation of Jesus' life from the point of view of faith. For this only those genres came into play for which meaning and interpretation could flow directly from faith. But this is exactly the function of the *historical narrative*. In contrast to mere reporting, it permits interpretation and exegesis to be part of its structure. It permits, with the help of individual narrative elements and with the help of the entire arrangement of them, the interpretation of history and its consideration from the experience of faith. It proceeds from real events but is not content to reproduce their external course. It never permits the connection with the historical-factual to be broken, but it accomplishes much more than just the enumeration of historical facts.

We have already said that in this mélange of communication and simultaneous interpretation of facts which constitutes the historical narrative the proportions can be unevenly distributed. Often the enumeration of facts is dominant, but the facts can also be much neglected in favor of interpretation. The latter is often the case in the New Testament. It can happen that a New Testament narrative is so intensely concerned with the inner meaning of Jesus' appearance on the scene and with the mystery of his person that it is far distant from the external historical course of events. In the following section we will turn to a typical narrative of this kind, the announcement of Jesus' birth.

—— 8 ——

The Annunciation of the Birth of Jesus

In the sixth month the angel Gabriel was sent by God to a town in Galilee called Nazareth, to a virgin betrothed to a man named Joseph, of the House of David; and the virgin's name was Mary. He went in and said to her, "Rejoice, so highly favored! The Lord is with you." She was deeply disturbed by these words and asked herself what this greeting could mean, but the angel said to her, "Mary, do not be afraid; you have won God's favor. Listen! You are to conceive and bear a son, and you must name him Jesus. He will be great and will be called the Son of the Most High. The Lord God will give him the throne of his ancestor David; he will rule over the House of Jacob forever and his reign will have no end." Mary said to the angel, "But how can this come about, since I am a virgin?" "The Holy Spirit will come upon you," the angel answered, "and the power of the Most High will cover you with its shadow. And so the child will be holy and will be called Son of God. Know this too: your kinswoman Elizabeth has, in her old age, herself conceived a son, and she whom people called barren is now in her sixth month, *for nothing is impossible to God*." "I am the handmaid of the Lord," said Mary, "let what you have said be done to me." And the angel left her.

[LUKE 1:26–38]

When we compare this narrative to that of the arrest of Jesus in Mark 14, we see at once that the very thing lacking here is what struck our notice there: the fragmentation and disunity of events—the accidental, insignificant, and basically trivial, as it is shown especially in the episode of the young man who had to flee naked.

In this text there is nothing accidental or trivial. Here everything has its deep meaning; here everything stands in an inner context. Nothing disturbs the unity and conciseness of what happens; everything unfolds in marvelous clarity. If one asks whence this clarity and transparency of the entire passage actually comes, one very soon discovers that the individual structural elements of the narrative have almost nothing historical and concrete about them.

Even the first words of our narrative are most instructive in this respect. At first the time indication "In the sixth month" seems to be very concrete, indeed something that could not be invented. In reality, however, it is a meaningful, illuminating narrative connection. It connects the annunciation of Jesus' birth with that of John's. At the end of the narrative we are expressly told that Elizabeth is already in the sixth month of her pregnancy. The sixth month at the beginning of the narrative then indicates the lapse of time since Gabriel's appearance to Zechariah. Why the sixth month is chosen for his coming to Mary is obvious. Elizabeth's pregnancy is to be for Mary a validating sign. But before the sixth month a pregnancy is not externally visible. And since Mary, in the continuation of the narrative, hastily prepares to visit Elizabeth, the announcement of Jesus' birth must by no means take place before Elizabeth's sixth month of pregnancy. The

Christian painters have always painted the Annunciation scene as vividly and concretely as it is told to us in Luke 1:26–38. But what is the real meaning of the text? Does it intend to give a historically factual account?

specification of time at the beginning of our text accordingly is not intended to set a concrete historical date but to associate the prehistory of Jesus with the prehistory of John.

But the constructive aspect of the narrative becomes even plainer when we know that the structural units of the conversation between Gabriel and Mary are largely derived from the Old Testament. They were already at the writer's disposal as fixed formulas.

"The Lord is with you" matches the words in Judges 6:12 spoken by the angel of the Lord when he appears before Gideon. "Do not be afraid" is a stereotypic form of address in the Old Testament when heavenly beings appear before humans—cf. Genesis 15:1; Joshua 8:1; Judges 6:23; Daniel 10:12; Tobit 12:17. "Nothing is impossible to God" parallels Genesis 18:14, "Is anything too wonderful for Yahweh?"—which, significantly, occurs in the context of the announcement of the birth of Isaac. Finally the sentences "He will be great and will be called the Son of the Most High. The Lord God will give him the throne of his ancestor David; he will rule over the House of Jacob forever and his reign will have no end" are a clear reference to the famous promise of Nathan in which God announces to David a successor for his throne and at the same time eternal dominion for his house (2 Samuel 7:12–16).

But this is not enough! Not only individual formulas of dialogue are derived from the Old Testament or refer to it. The constructive quality of our narrative becomes really clear only when the structure of the dialogue in its entirety is examined. It must, after all, be noticeable that the annunciation of John in Luke 1:5–20 and the annunciation of Jesus in this text follow exactly the same pattern:

1) a heavenly being appears;
2) the birth of a son is announced;
3) his name is determined;
4) his future is revealed.

From where does this pattern come, whose component parts and structure are by no means self-evident? The answer is simple and has long been known to biblical scholars: from the Old Testament. In numerous texts we find the same pattern when the birth of a child is predicted and proclaimed. It is called therefore simply "the pattern of proclamation."

Two examples should clarify the fact that what we have here is indeed a fixed pattern.

(1) In Genesis 16:7–12 the angel of God appears to Hagar, Sarah's maid, and announces to her the birth of a son:

"Now you have conceived, and you will bear a son,
and you shall name him Ishmael,
for Yahweh has heard your cries of distress.
A wild ass of a man he will be,
against every man, and every man against him,
setting himself to defy all his brothers."

[GENESIS 16:11–12]

(2) In Genesis 17:15–19 God appears to Abraham and announces to him, at first in general form, the birth of a son from Sarah. Abraham falls on his face and laughs. He thinks:

"Is a child to be born to a man one hundred years old, and will Sarah have a child at the age of ninety?"

Then God gives him the solemn assurance:

". . . your wife Sarah shall bear you a son whom you are to name Isaac. With him I will establish my Covenant, a covenant in perpetuity, to be his God and the God of his descendants after him."

The four component parts of the pattern of proclamation can be clearly recognized: God or his angel appears, the birth of a son is announced, his name is determined, his future or an important aspect of his future is revealed. The annunciation of John (Luke 1:13–17) and the annunciation of Jesus (Luke 1:31–33) follow this pattern very closely. The New Testament narrators must, then, have been familiar with corresponding Old Testament texts and must have carefully imitated their structure. Again a sign of the schematic and constructive nature of this narrative!

Now this pattern of proclamation explains structurally only half of the narrative. Next Mary intimates her doubts; the angel removes the doubts, and finally gives Mary a sign by which she can recognize that God is fulfilling his promise. Can an Old Testament pattern, already established, be shown to exist for this second part of the narrative?

Indeed it can. The granting of a sign by God is a fixed component of Old Testament narratives of vocation.

These call narratives are often constructed according to the following pattern:

1) God announces a call;
2) the one called expresses doubt;
3) God removes this doubt by an explanation;
4) God grants a sign in ratification of the call.

This Old Testament pattern, which we will call the "pattern of call" can be demonstrated by two characteristic passages.

(1) In Exodus 3:10–12 the mission of Moses to Pharaoh is narrated as follows. God says to Moses:

> ". . . so come, I send you to Pharaoh to bring the sons of Israel, my people, out of Egypt." Moses said to God, "Who am I to go to Pharaoh and bring the sons of Israel out of Egypt?" "I shall be with you," was the answer, "and this is the sign by which you shall know that it is I who have sent you . . . After you have led the people out of Egypt, you are to offer worship to God on this mountain."

(2) In Jeremiah the prophet describes his call by God. Although we have here a prophetic report in the first person, which differs in many ways from the narrative in Exodus 3, the same pattern underlies both. Only here the sign is not worked at some time in the future but immediately, by God.

> The word of Yahweh was addressed to me, saying,
>
> > "Before I formed you in the womb I knew you;
> > before you came to birth I consecrated you;
> > I have appointed you as prophet to the nations."
>
> I said, "Ah, Lord Yahweh; look, I do not know how to speak; I am a child!"
>
> > But Yahweh replied,
> > "Do not say, 'I am a child.'
> > Go now to those to whom I send you
> > And say whatever I command you.
> > Do not be afraid of them,
> > For I am with you to protect you—
> > it is Yahweh who speaks!"
>
> Then Yahweh put out his hand and touched my mouth and said to me:
>
> > "There! I am putting words into your mouth. . . ."
> >
> > [JEREMIAH 1:4–10]

It is obvious that in both Old Testament texts a fixed pattern is present, and that the second part of Luke 1:26–38 is constructed exactly according to this pattern. A formal *mission* of Mary is not there, for the proclamation narrative is not a call narrative. The mission is replaced by the announcement of the birth, the name, and the future of the child. Then, to be sure, the second structural unit is added, sharp and clear: Mary, like Jeremiah and Moses, expresses a doubt. This doubt, then, as the pattern requires, is canceled by Gabriel's explanation. And then the fourth structural unit follows, the ratifying sign: Mary will recognize, in the pregnancy of the aged Elizabeth, that God keeps his promises.

Clearly almost the entire narrative of Luke 1:26–38 is composed with the aid of the Old Testament. Not only are fixed formulas incorporated (such as "nothing is impossible to God"); the narrative even follows a precedent Old Testament pattern, or better, two Old Testament patterns combined.

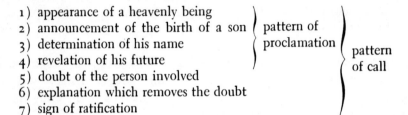

1) appearance of a heavenly being
2) announcement of the birth of a son ⎱ pattern of
3) determination of his name   ⎰ proclamation
4) revelation of his future   pattern
5) doubt of the person involved   of call
6) explanation which removes the doubt
7) sign of ratification

Only after we have uncovered thus the inner structure of the proclamation narrative can we say why it is so unified, clearly constructed, and transparent: It does not try to reproduce reality, with all its contradictions and accidents, but narrates on the basis of fixed structural laws and established elements of form, which are derived from the Old Testament.

So here we are much more remote from the genre of report or chronicle than in the narrative of Jesus' arrest. And we are compelled to draw the conclusion that the narrator is concerned here much less than there with communicating mere facts; his almost exclusive concern is with interpretation and exegesis. But what is to be interpreted? What is our narrative all about? What does it actually intend to state? Where does its center of meaning lie?

In the case of the pattern of proclamation the answer is not difficult. The fact that the narrative states that even before his birth a human being has been proclaimed by a heavenly being can only mean that the essence and salvific importance of this human being is to be shown. The center of meaning of the proclamation pattern must then lie in the last part, which reveals the future of the child.

The call pattern is exactly the reverse. There neither the announcement of the sign nor the explanation of God which clears up human doubt can be the high point; the two elements after all are not independent of each other but serve only to underline and to clarify God's calling, which has been issued in the first part of the pattern.

The central meaning of our narrative, then, can lie neither in Mary's expressed doubt (verse 34) nor in Gabriel's explanation (verse 35) nor in the ratifying sign announced to Mary (verses 36–37). Since in the call pattern the high point is to be found right in the first part, it must lie in the angel's message—even before Mary expresses her doubt. There again according to the structure of the proclamation pattern, neither the announcement of Jesus' birth nor the determination of his name but only the revelation of his future can form the central meaning.

Thus structural analysis shows unmistakably that the high point and the center of meaning of this passage lie in the sentences:

> "He will be great and will be called Son of the Most High. The Lord God will give him the throne of his ancestor David; he will rule over the House of Jacob forever and his reign will have no end."
>
> [LUKE 1:32–33]

Of course this is a most important, indeed decisive result. But before we evaluate it in detail, we must recall the question we asked. From the structural and schematic character of the proclamation narrative we drew the conclusion that its first concern was not to communicate facts but to give an interpretation. We then asked, What is to be interpreted in this narrative? Now, after we have realized, with the help of form criticism, which sentence is crucial, the answer to our question can only be: The person, essence, and mystery of Jesus is to be interpreted. We have a Christological narrative before us. It means that the child to be conceived by Mary will be called the Son of the Most High—that is, people will say of him that he is the *Son of God*. Furthermore, God will give him the throne of his father David—that is, Jesus will be installed as *Messiah*, and, as the text defines, for eternal dominion. Yes, when we consider that the pattern of proclamation begins as a narrative even before the birth in order to reveal the essence of a person, we must even formulate the actual statement of our narrative like this: Jesus *is* the Son of God; he *is* the Messiah; he *is* installed into his eternal dominion; in him the Messianic promises of the Old Testament have been fulfilled.

But all these are confessional statements of the post-Easter community about Jesus. In the New Testament there are numerous texts which show that "Son of God" and "Messiah" are central confessional statements of the primitive Church in which it sought to understand the mystery of Jesus crucified and risen. So we may say that a post-Easter confessional statement stands at the center of meaning of our narrative, not, to be sure, as an isolated confession but produced and formulated as narrative.

Now in Luke 1:26–38 the *conception of Jesus by the Spirit* also of course plays an important role. What value and function in the text does the statement have that Jesus was conceived without the co-operation of a man?

First of all it is clear that this statement is to receive special emphasis. Mary, after all, expresses a doubt, which is then removed by Gabriel's explanation. By this means a strong accent, from the point of view of narrative technique, is put upon the statement. On the other hand, it is obvious that Gabriel's explanation in verse 35 is not of equal value to the revelation of Jesus as the Messiah and Son of the Most High in verse 32. The explanation in verse 35 only underlines and clarifies the revelation of verse 32. Jesus is the Son of God, because he owes his human existence to God's creative act in the womb of a virgin. Just the form and structure of our narrative prove, then, that the statement of the conception of Jesus by the Spirit is not simply a statement equal in importance to that which says he is the Son of God. But another, quite different observation points in the same direction.

The confession that Jesus is the promised Messiah and the Son of God is found at all levels of the New Testament, from the oldest letter of Paul to the Gospel of John. It is a primordial matter of faith of the Church, alive in every community, and surfacing in many variations throughout the New Testament. On the other hand, the statement of the conception of Jesus by the Spirit is found only in this text and in Matthew 1:18–25. It is lacking in all the rest of the New Testament, and in the two texts in which it does appear, it is not a real confessional statement: It is not written for its own sake but both times has the function of underlining and clarifying that Jesus is the Son of God.

So we may really say that our narrative is Christological. At its center are post-Easter confessional statements. Jesus is the Son of God. Jesus is the Messiah, exalted to eternal dominion; Jesus is the fulfillment of Old Testament promises. In our narrative we are concerned with the emphasis and demonstration of these early confessional statements. So we would do well to speak of a "confessional narrative" when we define the genre. It states and confesses who Jesus was, by looking back to the time before Jesus' conception, and by narrating, with the help of Old Testament patterns, Jesus' beginnings. It states and confesses: Jesus is the Son of God, for he came from God.

If this is so, we naturally no longer have any possibility of investigating the Annunciation narrative on the basis of historical events—for example, whether Mary had a special experience of revelation or not. Of course there can have been such an experience. But it cannot be proven from Luke 1:26–38. The genre of narrative simply provides a jumping-off place for this.

Jesus is the Messiah; he is the Son of God; he is installed in his eternal lordship—this is the true sense of the Annunciation narrative. The confession of the post-Easter communities is projected back before the birth of Jesus in order to reveal his essence. (*Photo courtesy of Bildarchiv Foto, Marburg, Germany.*)

The narrative tells us only: Jesus is the Son of God, for his conception came to pass through the Spirit of God. It is silent about everything else. So it would simply be against the intent of the text to attempt to reconstruct a historical sequence of events. A further observation shows this to be impossible.

If our narrative were the reproduction of a real conversation between Gabriel and Mary, the objection of Mary that she had as yet no sexual relations with a man would be completely incomprehensible. For as a betrothed woman she could have understood the promise "You are to conceive and bear a son" only in the sense that she would conceive this child after being brought home by Joseph—that is, after the start of their marital life. Why then did she raise the question of her not having a sexual relationship with a man at all? One cannot evade this difficulty by assuming that Mary apparently referred the time of the announced conception to the time of her betrothal, thus to the time before she was married to Joseph. The promise of the angel could never have such a meaning for a Jewish girl on the threshold of marriage. Then there only remains the assumption that Mary at some time had taken a vow of virginity, and therefore could see no possibility of a pregnancy. This is the sense in which the surprised question of Mary to the angel has actually been understood for centuries. But this assumption also is completely off the track and long since discarded by biblical scholars. First of all there is not a word in our text of a vow of virginity; secondly, such a vow, given the esteem in which a fertile marriage was held by the Jews, would be completely improbable; thirdly, then Mary would have given a promise of marriage without saying a word to her betrothed about her vow. However we view the matter, if the conversation between Gabriel and Mary is supposed to have gone as narrated in Luke, one becomes involved in insuperable difficulties.

If, on the other hand, we are serious about the fact that the narrative is in accordance with an Old Testament pattern, for which, specifically, an objection of the receiver of the revelation and an explanation which cancels the objection are essential, all the problems are solved at once. For then Mary's objection is not one of the historical Mary, but the narrator's hint to the reader, who must be shown in this way how he is to understand Jesus as the Son of God, as was spoken of before. It is accordingly really not appropriate to read our narrative as a historical documentary report.

This can be clarified by yet another phenomenon. To Mary as well as to Zechariah the angel appears *in bodily form*. In the case of Zechariah he stands at the right of the altar of incense (Luke 1:11); in the case of Mary we must imagine that he enters her house (Luke 1:28). In the same way, however, the angel of the Lord appears before the shepherds (Luke 2:9) in the nativity story. We have therefore in the early chapters of Luke's Gospel

In the opening chapters of Luke angels always appear in bodily form; in the opening chapters of Matthew they always appear in a dream. From this alone we can tell that the apparition of angels is a biblical means of representation. Historical inferences are therefore all but impossible.

three passages in which angels appear, and every time they come in actual bodily form.

The interesting thing now is that in the early chapters of Matthew's Gospel an angel of the Lord also appears—in 1:20, 2:13, and 2:19. But here the appearances do not come as real, bodily entrances on the scene, but it is expressly noted in all three passages that the appearances took place in *dreams*. God sends the person a dream; in this dream the person sees an angel, and the angel tells the person what he should do. Both theologically and psychologically this is essentially more sublime than in Luke's Gospel.

Why do angels appear in Luke in bodily form and in Matthew in dreams? If we take the cited texts as historical reports, we must say that God sometimes caused angels to appear bodily, sometimes only in a dream; Luke by chance reports only the bodily appearances; Matthew, again by chance, only the dream appearances.

That this does not work is no doubt clear to every reader, especially when he finds out that even in the Old Testament there are quite varied descriptive forms for heavenly appearances: very realistic forms for narrators who otherwise are accustomed to write realistically, and theologically reserved descriptive forms for narrators who are accustomed to write in a theologically reserved manner. From this it follows very clearly that the very manner in which the angel appears in our narrative is a descriptive form. So we would do well, in narratives of this kind, to table all historical questions and concentrate on their actual *statements*. In this case the statement is: Jesus is the Son of God. Even his origin lies in God.

—— 9 ——

A Revelation Discourse

Similitude, instructive narrative, saga, historical narrative, report, confessional narrative—these are the various genres of narration in the Bible. Neither the attitude of the narrator nor the aim of the narrative nor the actual setting resemble each other. Of course there are in the Bible other ways of telling a story which have resulted in a larger number of genres. But we will stop here, in order to cast at least a glance at genres that do not tell the story of something that has happened but reproduce words and speeches. Of course here again the most varied genres and forms are possible. Let us select an example.

Every reader of the Gospels must have noted at some time or other that Jesus speaks differently in Matthew, Mark, and Luke than he does in John. Differently not only in content but also in form. In what does this difference consist, and how is it to be explained? Let us first consider a rather long passage of discourse in order to familiarize ourselves with the formal peculiarities of Jesus' speech as John records them. This passage comes from the eighth chapter and is directed at an inexactly defined group of listeners, among whom Pharisees are included.

When Jesus spoke to the people again, he said:

> "I am the light of the world;
> anyone who follows me will not be walking in the dark;
> he will have the light of life."

At this the Pharisees said to him, "You are testifying on your own behalf; your testimony is not valid." Jesus replied:

> "It is true that I am testifying on my own behalf,
> but my testimony is still valid,
> because I know
> where I came from and where I am going;
> but you do not know
> where I came from or where I am going.
> You judge by human standards;
> I judge no one,
> but if I judge,
> my judgment will be sound,
> because I am not alone:
> the one who sent me is with me;
> and in your Law it is written
> that the testimony of two witnesses is valid.
> I may be testifying in my own behalf,
> But the Father who sent me is my witness too."

They asked him, "Where is your Father?" Jesus answered:

> "You do not know me, nor do you know my Father;
> if you did know me, you would know my Father as well."

He spoke these words in the treasury, while teaching in the Temple. No one arrested him, because his time had not yet come.
Again he said to them:

> "I am going away; you will look for me
> and you will die in your sin.
> Where I am going, you cannot come."

The Jews said to one another, "Will he kill himself? Is that what he means by saying 'Where I am going you cannot come'?" Jesus went on:

> "You are from below;
> I am from above.
> You are of this world:

I am not of this world.
I have told you already: You will die in your sins.
Yes, if you do not believe that I am He,
you will die in your sins."

So they said to him, "Who are you?" Jesus answered:

"What I have told you from the outset.
About you I have much to say
and much to condemn;
but the one who sent me is truthful,
and what I have learned from him
I declare to the world."

They failed to understand that he was talking to them about the Father. So Jesus said:

"When you have lifted up the Son of Man,
then you will know that I am He
and that I do nothing of myself:
what the Father has taught me
is what I preach:
he who sent me is with me,
and has not left me to myself,
for I always do what pleases him."

As he was saying this, many came to believe in him.

[JOHN 8:12–30]

The first thing to strike our notice in this section of discourse from John's Gospel is the solemn introduction of himself at the beginning: "I am the light of the world." To this self-introduction a promise is immediately attached: "Anyone who follows me will not be walking in the dark; he will have the light of life." This connection between self-introduction (starting with "I am") and promise (starting with "anyone who") is often found in John's Gospel. Compare:

"I am the bread of life.
He who comes to me will never be hungry;
He who believes in me will never thirst."

[JOHN 6:35]

"I am the living bread which has come down from heaven.
Anyone who eats this bread will live forever;

[JOHN 6:51]

"I am the light of the world;
anyone who follows me will not be walking in the dark;
he will have the light of life."

[JOHN 8:12]

"I am the gate.
Anyone who enters through me will be safe . . ."

[JOHN 10:9]

"I am the resurrection and the life.
If anyone believes in me, he will live,
and whoever lives and believes in me
will never die."

[JOHN 11:25]

"I am the vine,
you are the branches.
Whoever remains in me, with me in him,
bears fruit in plenty."

[JOHN 15:5]

The countertest can now easily be made by investigating whether this fixed pattern exists also in the speeches of Jesus in the first three Gospels. The result is unequivocal: The pattern of self-introduction followed by a promise does not once occur in Jesus' words in the other three Gospels. Jesus' discourse in John 8:12–30, then, begins with a fixed pattern, lacking in the Synoptics but characteristic of John's Gospel. Actually only the Johannine Jesus speaks in this way.

But what is the nature of this discourse? What kind of linguistic form is it which begins with an introduction of self, continues with a promise, and then goes on as in John 8:12–29? To understand this better, let us first consider a passage not from the Bible but from the pagan philosopher Celsus (second century A.D.). Celsus, in his travels through Syria and Palestine, had listened to oriental itinerant preachers who appeared in the villages and cities and gave addresses to the crowds. They all told more or less the same story. Celsus summarizes the content of their preaching as follows:

"I am God or God's Son or divine Spirit. I have come, for the destruction of the world is imminent, and because of your misdeeds, O mankind, you are about to perish. But I will save you. Soon you will see me ascend with heavenly power. Blessed is he who now worships me! Upon all others I will cast eternal fire, on all cities and countries. And those who do not recognize that they are being punished will repent and groan in vain. But those who believe in me I will protect forever."[17]

In a comparison of this passage with Jesus' discourses in John's Gospel, the differences should first be emphasized strongly. They are serious. Nowhere in John's Gospel does Jesus speak in such a primitive, bombastic, and arrogant way of himself and his mission. In John Jesus nowhere says, "I am God," but he does say, "To have seen me is to have seen the Father" (John

So spoke, according to Celsus' portrayal, the wandering preachers of the ancient Near East. In the Gospels Jesus never says, "I am God." He also never speaks in so bombastic and explicit a manner about himself and his mission. However, in the Gospel of John the same form—that of the revelation discourse—is to be found. How can this phenomenon be explained?

14:9). He asks no one to adore him, but he does challenge us to believe that he is sent by God.

> "Whoever believes in me
> believes not in me
> but in the one who sent me. . . ."
>
> [JOHN 12:44]

Finally he demands belief not first of all from fear of eternal punishment, as in the pagan text, but so that people may attain to knowledge of the truth and find true life.

> "I have come so that they may have life,
> and have it to the full."
>
> [JOHN 10:10]

A comparison with the Celsus passage shows, indeed, that the Jesus of John's Gospel does not belong in the long series of ancient thaumaturges and itinerant preachers who pretended to be gods in human form and tried to spellbind the crowds with magic and threatening sermons.

Despite these profound differences in content, however, the common features of form are immediately noticeable. The Celsus passage, like John 8:12–29, also begins with a self-introduction of the speaker which, as in John, it is couched in the "I am" form. In both cases this self-introduction is basically a self-revelation—that is, a self-revelation with absolute claims. One cannot question it closely. It can only be accepted or rejected. In the Gospel of John, to be sure, this absoluteness of self-revelation is expressed even more plainly than in the short passage of Celsus. For in John the Pharisees reproach Jesus with giving witness for himself—an unreliable witness. When Jesus replies to this that his father also gives witness for him, the absoluteness of his self-revelation is not removed, for the Father's witness is given only to whoever believes in Jesus (cf. verse 19). The claim of Jesus, accordingly, is not to be questioned; therefore he can always only phrase it differently. For this reason he says again and again, "I am He!" (cf. 8:24, 28).

With this absolute claim Jesus becomes a crisis. That is, he becomes the one who divides the world. He separates himself from his hearers:

> "You are from below;
> I am from above.
> You are of this world;
> I am not of this world."
>
> [JOHN 8:23]

At the same time he divides his listeners—into those who believe in him and those who do not. To this division of his hearers into believers and nonbelievers corresponds the juxtaposition of promise and threat in the discourse. In the Celsus passage the parallelism of threat and promise is especially clear. There we find even the double construction:

"Blessed is he who worships me" [promise].
"Upon all others I will cast eternal fire" [threat].
"And those who do not recognize that they are being punished, will repent in vain" [threat].
"But those who believe in me I will protect forever" [promise].

Thus we have promise, threat, threat, promise, as in the structure A-B-B-A.

Jesus' discourse also contains a solemn promise, but adds it, characteristically, immediately to the self-introduction:

"I am the light of the world;
anyone who follows me will not be walking in the dark;
he will have the light of life."

Nor is a threat lacking; it is not expressed, however, until 8:24:

"Yes, if you do not believe that I am He,
you will die in your sins."

Again let us point to the deep difference in content between the threat in Jesus' discourse and the threat of the Celsus text. Here, to be sure, we are interested only in the actual presence of the threat.

Summarizing, we can say that in both John 8:12–29 and the Celsus passage we have a form of discourse in which the speaker puts his claim absolutely and unquestionably before his hearers. With his discourse he covers the world situation and proclaims that there is only one possibility to save oneself—to believe in him. The self-introduction of the speaker and the duplication of promise and threat are typical of this form of discourse. The whole genre of discourse could be briefly described as "revelation discourse of a redeemer." The individual elements and characteristic signs of this genre are found in many other of Jesus' discourses in John's Gospel.

But whence come the similarities of form in the discourse of oriental itinerant preachers sketched in Celsus and Jesus' discourses in the Gospel of John? Did Celsus, or perhaps the men he encountered in Palestine, consciously imitate John's Gospel and use it for a model of discourse? Such a solution is wildly improbable, for the type of revelation discourse here described was in widespread use in the ancient world as early as the first and second century of our era. We encounter it in many documents of the time which discuss mysteries, revelations, secret knowledge, and wisdom. Thus, for example, at the beginning of our century the extremely ancient writings of the Mandaeans were discovered. These were an Eastern Syrian sect of baptists, whose origins reach back into the first century. In these documents there are numerous revelation discourses with exactly the same form elements as we found in the Gospel of John and in Celsus. This then is how the "Revealer" introduces himself in the "John Book" of the Mandaeans:

> "I am a fisherman of the great life, of the mighty life, of the great life, a messenger whom life has sent. Beware of the world! Beware of the stinking birds that are above you! If you take heed and beware, my brothers, I will help you. I will be a help and a support from the place of darkness to the place of light."[18]

In another document of the Mandaeans, *The Real Ginza*, the Revealer speaks:

> "I am the envoy of the light; everyone who smells its fragrance will receive life. Everyone who receives his words into himself, will have his eyes filled with light. But the evil ones, they, the liars, condemn themselves. The evil ones sink by their own will into the great sea of Sûf."[19]

Here too we have an unequivocal type of revelation discourse. The elements of form—self-introduction, promise, threat (or warning)—are at once recognizable. If I quoted these two Mandaean texts in their entirety, then even further similarities of form to John 8:12–29 would appear. But I want to confine myself to the elements of self-introduction–promise–threat. Even so, the nature of a revelation discourse has no doubt become plain. Now we must work out, above all, the differences in Jesus' manner of speaking as recorded in the Synoptic Gospels. For this we choose a text from Luke which is well suited for a comparison, for it contains likewise a rather long speech of Jesus, and this speech too demands radical decision from those who hear it:

> "I have come to bring fire to the earth, and how I wish it were blazing already! There is a baptism I must still receive, and how great is my distress till it is over!
> "Do you suppose that I am here to bring peace on earth? No, I tell you, but rather division. For from now on a household of five will be divided: three against two and two against three; the father divided

against the son, son against father, mother against daughter, daughter against mother, mother-in-law against daughter-in-law, daughter-in-law against mother-in-law."

He said again to the crowds, "When you see a cloud looming up in the west you say at once that rain is coming, and so it does. And when the wind is from the south you say it will be hot, and so it is. Hypocrites! You know how to interpret the face of the earth and the sky. How is it you do not know how to interpret these times?

"Why not judge for yourselves what is right? For example: when you go to court with your opponent, try to settle with him on the way, or he may drag you before the judge and the judge hand you over to the bailiff and the bailiff have you thrown in prison. I tell you, you will not get out until you have paid the very last penny.'"

[LUKE 12:49–59]

The profound stylistic difference between this speech of Jesus and the one in John strikes our notice at once. In John 8:12–29 Jesus is constantly interrupted by his audience. They keep making objections, asking questions, or showing their lack of understanding. And this very lack of understanding, as well as the objections and questions, carries the discourse on. Thus, from sentence to sentence a real progression of thought results, although the whole discourse is centered ultimately around the absolute, unquestionable claim of Jesus: "I am He!"

In the discourse in Luke this is all quite different. Objections or questions from the audience are here completely lacking. There is no developing context; there is no logical progression of thought. The basic theme for the whole discourse indeed is the thought of radical decision, which must be made now, at the moment when Jesus is speaking. This theme, however, is not progressively developed but is expressed anew in various single statements. If we look clearly, we see that Jesus' discourse in reality consists of five individual fragments, which are understandable in themselves and connected only subsequently:

1) a saying about fire (12:49),
2) a saying about baptism (12:50),
3) a saying about division (12:51–53),
4) a saying about weather (12:54–56),
5) a similitude about going to court (12:57–59).

By the constant change of the sources of imagery, which originally were unconnected, it is easily seen that we have here in fact five quite discrete sayings or fragments of discourse. First he speaks of fire, then baptism, then division in families, then changes in the weather; then finally he takes up

134

the situation in a court appearance. It is clear that sayings with such varying sources of imagery can be spoken only on very different occasions and never in the same context.

For this there are further proofs. For example, in the saying about the weather the audience is addressed in the plural: "When you see clouds in the west arising . . ." On the other hand, they are addressed in the next passage, the court scene, in the singular: "When you go to court, . . ." It becomes plain from this change in the style of address that separate fragments were welded together here later.

If we wish to understand the profound difference between Jesus' discourses in John and Luke, we must put the question of form more exactly. We have seen that John 8:12–29 belongs to the genre of revelation discourse, because here self-introduction, threat, and promise play a special role and the absolute claim of the speaker is constantly in the background. How is it with Luke? To what genre does Luke 12:49–59 belong? The answer can only be that Jesus' discourse in Luke is a secondary composition of separate sayings, which first existed independently. And these independent sayings belong to quite different genres. For example, in verse 49 there is a prophetic saying in the first person, in which Jesus speaks of his mission. In verses 52–53 we find the genre of foretelling the future, and finally in verses 58–59 that of the similitude. The whole discourse, then, is a composition or collage of different genres, which either belong to the area of prophetic speech or are close to it. But the revelation discourse is totally alien to the area of prophecy. In fact, Luke 12:49–59 has nothing at all to do with a revelation discourse either. There is, to be sure, a threat (verse 59), but no promise. And although in the saying about fire, for instance, he speaks of himself, there is no self-introduction as is typical in revelation discourse but a prophetic saying, with which Jesus outlines his mission. In this saying he says not who he is but whereunto he is sent. He speaks not as a revealer but as a prophet. The sentence in Luke "I have come to bring fire to the earth" is on a very different level from the statement in John "I am the light of the world."

In Luke 12:49–59 the Jesus of the first person remains in the background or very quickly recedes into the background. In the saying about the weather and the similitude of the court scene Jesus himself does not appear at all. The actual subject of the whole discourse is not Jesus but God. The audience is to understand what the message is about. The kingdom of God is at hand. Man has no more time. He must turn himself around. He must decide: for or against the kingdom of God. He must understand the challenge of the hour, comprehend the signs of the times. He has just as little time as a man on his way to see the judge. He can still settle out of court. But once the litigation has begun, it is too late. So quick action is in order.

How does it happen, Jesus asks his audience, that they can interpret the weather signs so well but cannot understand the signs which herald the approach of the kingdom of God? And the nearness of God's dominion requires man's total decision. Jesus knows that he is sent to bring about this decision. His message causes division and separation. It splits all relationships and connections. It is as effective as fire.

All of Jesus' sayings in Luke 12:49–59 speak of the present state of affairs in the light of the approaching dominion of God. Although this concept is not once named, it forms the background of the entire discourse. Jesus speaks as the herald of the incipient dominion of God. He sounds the call for decision in favor of God's kingdom, and therewith for God.

Only against this background does the special nature of the revelation discourse of John 8 become really visible. The Jesus of John does not point to what presses on us from the future but speaks of the present. He appears not as prophet but as revealer. With persistence and emphasis he puts his own person in the foreground. And note that this is true not only for the passage we have discussed but for the subject matter of all the discourses in John's Gospel. Again and again we encounter in the Fourth Gospel the genre of the revelation discourse, whereas prophetic forms of discourse unequivocally recede in importance. In contrast, the situation in the first three Gospels is the reverse: There prophetic forms of discourse predominate and the genre of revelation discourse is altogether absent.

In what way did the real Jesus speak? Like the Jesus of the Synoptics or like the Jesus of John? Formerly it was sometimes asserted that Jesus spoke as prophet *and* as revealer, but as revealer only in very specific situations; these situations are the ones handed down to us in the Fourth Gospel alone. But such a solution is completely out of the question—if only because most revelation discourses of John's Gospel are directed not to an esoteric audience but to the public. So we must decide: Either Jesus spoke as in John or he spoke as in the Synoptics.

Now for biblical scholarship this question has long since been decided, unquestionably and finally. For the Gospel of John is very different from the Synoptics not only in the genre of the revelation discourse but in its whole style. And this characteristic style of the Fourth Gospel is encountered, interestingly enough, not only in the discourse portions but in the whole Gospel and, even beyond this, in the First Epistle of John. Furthermore, the Gospel of John, in contrast to the Synoptics, has not only its own style but also its own pattern of themes, which is found again in the First Epistle. The author of this letter speaks about the same themes as the Jesus of John, and in the same style.

"Yes, God loved the world so much
that he gave his only Son,
so that everyone who believes in him
    may not be lost
but may have eternal life.
For God sent his Son into the world
not to condemn the world,
but so that through him the world
    might be saved."

[JOHN 3:16–17]

God's love for us was revealed
when God sent into the world his only
    Son
so that we could have life through him;
this is the love I mean:
not our love for God,
but God's love for us when he sent
    his Son
to be the sacrifice that takes our sins
    away.

[1 JOHN 4:9–10]

The conclusions are inescapable: Behind the Fourth Gospel and the First Epistle of John stands a really great theologian—probably with a circle of disciples—who causes Jesus to speak in his own manner. Also, in the three oldest Gospels we are closer to the historical Jesus than in the Gospel of John. Moreover, the revelation discourse in John 8:12–29 is the composition of an early Christian theologian, not a discourse of the historical Jesus.

All these conclusions are inescapable for the historian and long since the general property of biblical scholarship. But these conclusions are insufficient. Whoever meets these conclusions and says nothing further is not yet telling the whole truth. For we must ask in this case also, just as in the narrative material of the Bible, does truth consist only in the correctness of external facts, or are there other quite different forms of truth? Concretely, does a discourse of Jesus reproduce what he was and what he intended only when it is like a tape recording of his words, or can it be formed from secondary sources and in a very free manner and still reproduce what he was and what he intended? Even more concretely, could it be that Jesus never spoke in the form of a revelation discourse, and that nonetheless the revelation discourses of John reproduce exactly what Jesus was in the deepest part of his being and exactly what he intended?

We saw that Jesus used prophetic forms of discourse; that he did not proclaim himself but, like a prophet, pointed to God and the dawning of God's dominion. From this it would be logical to designate Jesus a prophet and to seek the actual mystery of his person in the prophetic. Actually Jesus was first interpreted in this way. Compare Luke 7:16:

Everyone was filled with awe and praised God, saying, "A great prophet has appeared among us; God has visited his people."

Photography and drawing are two representational forms that reveal different aspects of a subject. The two are to be distinguished but not opposed. In the same way, it makes no sense to play off the representation of Jesus offered in the first three Gospels

against that offered in the Gospel of John. For that matter, the comparison limps from the very start, for even the first three Gospels do not offer a "photograph" of Jesus. (*Photo by Rolf Bruderer. Drawing by Larry Schwinger.*)

But correct as it is to find in what Jesus did and said a multitude of prophetic elements, the question yet remains whether in this way the mystery of his person is really described.

Even the eschatological character of Jesus' preaching cannot be entirely adequately captured with the concept of the prophetic. Jesus does not wish only to interpret a specific stage in Israel's development from the divine point of view, but he proclaims that now the ultimate action of God has begun. He proclaims that now God is speaking his last and irrevocable word, ultimately causing his salvation and judgment to begin, and that therefore the hour of radical decision has come.

It is true that we could here refer to John the Baptist, whose preaching likewise was eschatological in nature. But Jesus not only understands his preaching as the final, ultimate word of God, but also attaches to his preaching the claim that all the promises of the Old Testament are fulfilled in the hour of his appearance. Thus he can say:

"Happy the eyes that see what you see, for I tell you that many prophets and kings wanted to see what you see, and never saw it; to hear what you hear, and never heard it."

[LUKE 10:23–24]

If one asks what Jesus really means by what was not possible to hear and see before but now *is* possible to see and hear, the answer can only be that he means the cures he brings about; he means his exorcisms of demons and his powerful preaching; he means the fellowship he maintains with tax-collectors and sinners. In all this the promises are being fulfilled; in all this the dominion of God is at its dawn. But this implies also that Jesus considers his entire activity as a great sign by which the power and glory of God's approaching dominion are already becoming visible. The message of Jesus therefore cannot ever be separated from his person. Basically Jesus considers himself to be the sign of the time and the sign of the coming glory of God. But this, tacitly and implicitly, presupposes an unheard-of self-consciousness, in which everything prophetic is far surpassed.

But even so, not everything is said. Above all, one must heed the manner in which Jesus makes God's will operative. Not by book-learning or the lore of sages, but also not in the manner of the prophets, who appeared before the people with God's words as transmitted to them. The familiar formula "thus speaks Yahweh," with which the prophets of the Old Testament introduced their message, does not once appear in Jesus' words. He replaces the Old Testament heraldic formula with a sentence uniquely His own: "Amen, I say unto you" (translated, "I tell you solemnly," in the Jerusalem Bible). From this sentence there speaks a momentous and, for a

Jew, unprecedented awareness of full power. Jesus is not transmitting God's words that he has received, like the prophets, but dares to speak as if he himself stood in God's place.[20]

We will stop here, for it is hardly our function to investigate in detail the self-consciousness of Jesus underlying his actions and his words. We can only indicate that Jesus' claim to supreme power transcends by far the framework and the potential of the prophetic. Underlying his words and deeds a consciousness of self is concealed that evades all obvious, superficial definitions and by far exceeds the limits of what was possible then in Judaism.

The writer of the Gospel of John endeavors to comprehend this power-consciousness of Jesus by means of the concept of the revealer and the genre of the revelation discourse; that is a bold and splendid attempt to grasp and express the claim which underlies Jesus' appearance. For if one looks more closely, one recognizes that the writer of the Fourth Gospel only continues to contemplate what is hinted at in the words of Jesus in the first three Gospels, that he only extends the lines already drawn, and that he only develops a picture already in sketch form. Thus behind the "I am He" of John's Gospel stands the claim of Jesus expressed in "Amen, I say to you." Behind the sentence of John's Jesus "To have seen me is to have seen the Father" stands the fact that the historical Jesus regarded his works and himself as the sign of the dawning dominion of God. And behind the words of threat and promise in the Johannine revelation discourses stands the call for decision which Jesus issued because of the imminent end of all things.

Anyone trying to obtain some sense of literary forms must sometimes be alarmed at the profound difference between Jesus' manner of speaking in the Synoptics on the one hand and in John on the other. But the same observer, as soon as he looks closer and listens more attentively, will recognize how exactly and faithfully, despite all differences, the Gospel of John illuminates what Jesus actually was.

It comes down to this: In John's Gospel it is not simply the historical Jesus who speaks. The revelation discourses of this Gospel are meditations of a theologian of the early Church concerning Jesus' message and the mystery of his person. But they are meditations and reflections of the greatest New Testament theologian, after Paul—sustained by faith in Christ and by a deep love. And can then the mystery of a person be otherwise known than by ever more fervent meditation and ever renewed total commitment?

10

The Statement on Divorce

Hitherto all of our form-critical investigations into concrete passages of scripture have ended again and again with the question: historical or not? That is, form and genre criticism have turned out to be a decisive help in determining whether an event really took place, whether words were really spoken, in just the way the biblical passage led us to expect. From all of this a false impression could very easily arise that form criticism is the proper method of distinguishing between what is historical and what is not. Actually this would be asking too much of the discipline. Of course in many cases it can be shown with the help of form criticism that an event has certainly *not* taken place in the way described. But this is not a decision in principle about the historicity of the event. For it could be that an author used an already established descriptive form for the reproduction of real facts. In this case the conclusion *a posteriori* from a fixed form pattern to the nonhistoricity of the subject matter reproduced would be dangerous.

Let us then emphatically assert: Form and genre criticism can never by themselves decide historical questions. The real function of form criticism is elsewhere: It is supposed to help uncover the aim and intent of a text. It is supposed to show what a text actually aims at, where its focus of meaning lies, and what kind of language it speaks. Form criticism must accordingly also be applied where there is no primary interest in establishing historicity. Let us clarify this by means of some examples from the preaching of Jesus.

In Matthew 22:14 there is a saying attributed to Jesus: "Many are called, but few are chosen." Before we attempt a form-critical investigation of this sentence, there are a few preliminary problems to clear up. "Many" is not used here in contrast with "all." As often happens in Semitic languages, it has inclusive significance and means "the many," "the uncountable number," "all." For "called" we must think of God as the practical subject, as well as for "chosen." And by this "choosing" no predestinative action of God is meant, but the moment when men are taken up to eternal salvation—i.e., saved. The whole sentence means, then: "All men are called by God to eternal salvation, but only a few will achieve it."

As soon as the external sense of this sentence has been made clear, particular difficulties at once crop up. Is this word of Jesus not dreadful and discouraging? If only a few of the whole number of mankind are saved, it is most improbable that we should belong to this small number. Jesus' saying in Matthew 22:14 must accordingly lead to deep pessimism any person who takes it seriously, unless—and this is the point—he pays attention to its form.

The sentence is formulated as a sharp antithesis. Two pairs of words are juxtaposed:

all / few

called / saved

Such antitheses, which with great finesse place in contrast two related facts, are common enough elsewhere in Jesus' preaching. Compare:

> "Enter by the narrow gate, since the road that leads to perdition is wide and spacious, and many take it; but it is a narrow gate and a hard road that leads to life, and only a few find it."
>
> [MATTHEW 7:13–14]

> "Yes, I tell you again, it is easier for a camel to pass through the eye of a needle than for a rich man to enter the kingdom of heaven."
>
> [MATTHEW 19:24]

Common to these three sayings of Jesus are the short, concise form, the antithetical juxtaposition of related facts, and the sharp finesse. From this basic determination we must further ask what the linguistic intent of such concise, antithetical, and extremely pointed sentences really is. We have already seen that our language can pursue a variety of intents. It can

inform	confess	summon
instruct	adjure	admonish
discuss	assure	command
report	proclaim	forbid
narrate	lament	create community
describe	accuse	disrupt community
praise	challenge	

What is the linguistic intent in the sentences cited above? Certainly not to present or discuss a factual situation objectively, else the speaker would not grope for such extreme images and antitheses. Nor does he intend to praise, confess, or accuse. His actual goal is neither to create nor to disrupt community but, unequivocally, to admonish and to summon. Nor must we overlook the factor of challenge. In Jesus' extremely pointed formulation "easier for a camel to pass through the eye of a needle" he shakes up his listeners and disquiets them. His word becomes an axe that shatters the frozen armor of human indifference. His aim in this is for his audience to come to their senses and be converted.

So Jesus intends, with the intrinsically dreadful words "only a few will be saved," not to bring his hearers to despair nor to reject them but to shake them up and bring them to conversion. He intends to tell them, "Do not be called in vain! Be converted and do everything you can to belong to those chosen!" The words of Matthew 22:14 have prophetic, not informative character; they make no statistical statement as to the quantitative relationship of those saved to those lost, but they aim at shaking the listeners and tearing them loose from their perilous indifference.

Basically the Church has always, with complete correctness, assigned to these texts a provocative intent to convert. The Church never thought of stating as a principle of belief "Only a few will be saved" or "No rich man will enter heaven" on the basis of these passages. In this case, without much thought about it, the Church has, with correct intuition, determined the genre of a specific group of Jesus' sayings.

But nonetheless there are cases where such determination was more difficult, and where it was really not understood in what genre of discourse and with what intent Jesus had spoken. For several decades it has become more and more clear that this is so with Jesus' statement about divorce. Let us now turn our attention to this text.

Jesus' words about divorce are found in the most varied places in the New Testament and at the most varied levels of tradition. Compare 1 Corinthians 7:10–11; Mark 10:11–12; Luke 16:18; Matthew 5:32; and Matthew 19:9. The actual words in the passages cited all differ among each other indeed—a plain sign that the primitive Church was constantly concretizing these words of Jesus, and constantly adapting itself to the prevalent social situation.

Probably the oldest tradition is found in Matthew 5:32:

". . . everyone who divorces his wife, except for the case of fornication, makes her an adulteress; and anyone who marries a divorced woman commits adultery."

In this text the phrase "except for fornication" is a secondary addition to the tradition before or contemporary with Matthew. Its exact meaning is

"It is easier for a camel to pass through the eye of a needle than for a rich man to enter the kingdom of heaven." A saying that in this way is exaggerated in the extreme is not aiming at objective information but at challenge and confrontation. It is in just such sayings that the linguistic intention must be most exactly attended to.

still disputed. It is certain, however, that this so-called "fornication clause" is not from Jesus, for neither Mark, Luke, nor Paul records it. Here we can disregard it. Thus the original words were:

> "Everyone who divorces his wife makes her an adulteress, and anyone who marries a divorced woman commits adultery."

What do these words mean? They are correctly understood only when one knows Jewish matrimonial law. What is remarkable about this law is that it allows divorce in the most liberal fashion. The man is allowed to divorce his wife even if

> "she has not pleased him and he has found some impropriety in her."
> [DEUTERONOMY 24:1]

With this vague formulation many possibilities stood open—at least from the point of view of the law—to break the marriage with his wife. A divorce judge did not need to be consulted; it was enough for the man to present his wife with a writ of divorce. It is important to note that only the man could divorce. The wife could not serve a writ of divorce on her husband.

Other aspects of Jewish law show how unequally the wife was treated. Thus a man who had intercourse with another woman did not by any means break his own marriage; at most, if the woman was married to someone else, he broke her husband's marriage. How different with the wife! According to Jewish concepts she broke her own marriage by committing adultery. This is where it becomes plain that the wife was regarded not as a partner but as a piece of her husband's property; he possessed over her an almost material right of disposal. By her adultery she diminished, so to speak, her husband's possessions; he, however, by his adultery, could at most diminish the possessions of another husband.

Only if one heeds this social background can one understand why Jesus formulates his saying about divorce from the point of view of the man: "Everyone who divorces his wife makes her an adulteress, and anyone who marries a divorced woman commits adultery." After all, the wife did not have the right anyway to divorce her husband. Jesus therefore turns to the man. He shows him: Whoever divorces his wife forces her to look for another husband, because otherwise economic survival is impossible for her. So with the new husband she breaks her first marriage, and for this her first husband is to blame, for by his divorce he has driven her to this course. But the new husband also commits adultery—in reference to the first marriage, which was terminated by divorce.

To us this whole argument seems very complicated and circumstantial, especially in the first part. But Jesus formulated his saying in this way because according to the Jewish concept of legality the man could not commit adultery in respect to his own marriage. Defined accurately, to be sure, Jesus' words here are not an argument. He adduces no proofs. He calls that which was allowed to every Jew by the Mosaic law adultery, pure and simple. But for the Jews adultery was regarded as a great injustice, indeed as a capital crime, to be prosecuted, to which the death penalty was assigned. If Jesus therefore simply equates divorce and adultery, it must have meant a tremendous provocation for his audience, even sharper and harder than when he said to the rich, "A camel will come through the eye of a needle sooner than you into God's kingdom."

Why does Jesus put divorce, legally allowed for every Jewish man, on the level of adultery? His goal can only be to unmask ostensible righteousness as the most profound unrighteousness. Jesus is saying to his audience, "Formally you can invoke the law in matters of divorce, but in reality you are masking, with this legal right, a crying injustice. In appearance you can invoke God's law in divorce, but in reality you conceal his will. For God desires partnership between man and wife. Both, after all, are *one* flesh." By His provocative words Jesus defends the wife, for she has been delivered to her husband's arbitrary will—without any rights—and has been debased to the status of a thing. He defends the real will of God, which is falsified by human tradition and human statutes and is no longer recognizable in its original intention. Jesus has done this often before, as when he remonstrated to the Scribes and Pharisees:

> "How ingeniously you get round the commandment of God in order to preserve your own tradition! For Moses said: *Do your duty to your father and mother*, and, *Anyone who curses father or mother must be put to death*. But you say, 'If a man says to his father or mother: Anything that I have that I might have used to help you is Corban (that is, dedicated to God), then he is forbidden from that moment to do anything for his father or mother.' In this way you make God's word null and void for the sake of your tradition which you have handed down. And you do many other things like this."
>
> [MARK 7:9–13]

Like the wife in Matthew 5:32, parents are here defended against the Jewish practice of the law, and (as in the same text) the actual will of God is simultaneously demonstrated. The only difference is that in the case of the ban on divorce the provocation is much greater, for here Jesus turns not only against the law of Jewish custom but against the Mosaic law itself. He opposes his own word to the Mosaic law.

But in what form does he actually accomplish this? Is he setting up a new law, the law of the indissolubility of marriage? That is how his words on divorce have been understood for centuries: Jesus determined and arranged the indissolubility of marriage as the lawgiver of the New Covenant.

It is easy to understand why the words of Jesus on divorce have been interpreted in this sense as a law. They are, formally, couched unequivocally in terms of a legal principle. Legal principles of the pattern "To everyone who acts in such and such a way, such and such a thing will happen" are frequently encountered in the Bible and the ancient East. As early as in Genesis 9:6, we read:

> He who sheds man's blood,
> shall have his blood shed by man.

In this principle the first clause is the *definition of the facts of the case*, and the second clause the *determination of legal consequences*. In the Old Testament there are, however, also principles of law expressed according to the pattern "Everyone who does such and such a thing has made himself guilty." In such cases the second clause is not the determination of legal consequences but *declaration of guilt*. Compare Leviticus 17:3-4; Leviticus 20:9, 11, 12, 13, 16, 27; Numbers 35:16, 17, 18, 20ff. The text Matthew 5:32 is formed according to this second pattern. At first the facts of the case are defined in the first clause. Then, in the second clause, these facts are declared to be grievous guilt—namely, adultery. Thus no doubt can exist that Jesus' words about divorce are *formally* a principle of law in Matthew 5:32.

But is it therefore also *according to its intention* a principle of law? Does Jesus really intend to fix the law or set up new ones? We saw already that he is expressing a tremendous provocation by equating divorce and adultery. In this way he intends to shake people up, to unmask them, to uncover the true circumstances of Jewish divorce customs. But none of this is at all fitting for a law, because a law, if it is to be accepted, must never evoke resentment. Thus it seems likely that Jesus, in the words of Matthew 5:32 plays externally with the form of the legal statement, but expressly not to promulgate a new law; on the contrary his intention is to unmask the legal system of his contemporaries and to expose its absurdities. His words on divorce would then in reality be not legislation but prophetic discourse. It is typical of prophetic discourse to use strange genres and to change their actual setting. We saw this in the genre of the funeral song, which was often taken up by Old Testament prophets, who changed its function to a song of derision. Similarly Jesus would here have used the external form of the legal decision in order to arouse attention and shake up his hearers and thus express his actual concern.

That this is really so is shown by glancing at the context surrounding the text on divorce. Just the sentences about anger, which are couched much more unequivocally in the form of the legal decision, show that Jesus is not concerned with laying down the law. Let us look at these sentences in their entirety:

"You have learned how it was said to our ancestors: *You must not kill*; and if anyone does kill he must answer for it before the court. But I say this to you: anyone who is angry with his brother will answer for it before the court; if a man calls his brother 'Fool' he will answer for it before the Sanhedrin; and if a man calls him 'Renegade' he will answer for it in hell fire."

[MATTHEW 5:21–22]

In this series of sayings a tremendous sharpening of the law is observable from sentence to sentence. Formerly, says Jesus, it was like this: Whoever committed murder was condemned by the court—he means the local court. But now, from this moment, the procedure will be more strict. Now everyone who is angry at someone else even in his *heart* will be judged by the local court. And whoever says to another, "Fool!" will be condemned by the High Council. And whoever says, "Renegade" is damned to hell. It is clear that here he is speaking in precise legal phraseology and yet he has no intention at all of making a law. For what local court could pursue a man's inner anger, or how could the High Council in Jerusalem bother itself about verbal insults? Jesus uses the form of the legal principle to impress, unforgettably and unmistakably, upon his audience that death-dealing violence and aggression start not at the scene of a murder but long before, in the heart, with the first vituperative word, however harmless it seems. Therefore man should resist the first stirring of anger in his heart.

The same thing is true of adultery. It begins, if we listen to the Sermon on the Mount, not just when adultery is physically consummated but as soon as the first lustful glances are exchanged (cf. Matthew 5:27–28).

The same thing is true of perjury. Not only is perjury evil, but even the fact that oaths must be taken at all. Man should live in accordance with a mental attitude of absolute veracity, so that oaths become completely superfluous (cf. Matthew 5:33–37).

In all these instances—the ban on anger, lustful glances, and oaths—Jesus is speaking in the language of the law. And yet everyone realizes that no new laws are here to be promulgated. Nor did the Church ever think of deriving laws from the prohibition of anger, of lustful glances, or of oaths. Nor did it at any time get the idea of making a legal principle out of Jesus' demand for absolute relinquishment of power. Not only would such laws,

149

for reasons pertaining to the general welfare, be impossible and absurd! Even if they were possible, they could not achieve what Jesus wanted. Jesus' intention with the Sermon on the Mount surpasses every legality. He wants purity of heart, inner truth, absolute nonviolence, which would rather offer the other cheek than seek satisfaction. In all of this, man, long before he can get entangled with a law, is claimed and challenged by the will of God.

Precisely within this context, which we know familiarly as the Sermon on the Mount, there stands the prohibition of divorce. It has the same linguistic structure as the prohibition of oaths, lustful glances, and anger—and the same linguistic intent. Jesus is causing provocation also in his saying on divorce. Using legal terminology, he calls divorce a capital crime, worthy of death. But it is not his intention to issue a law on the indissolubility of marriage but to uncover its actual reality, which reaches deeper than any law and which can never be sufficiently protected by laws. With his words on divorce Jesus intends to force his hearers with ultimate severity to recognize the injustice of their divorce customs. But at the same time he wants to summon the husband to partnership with his wife, and he wants to bring him to that absolute unshakable love and fidelity which God means by marriage. His words are provocative, but in the final analysis provocative toward the good, toward the actual will of God.

Once we have grasped the linguistic intent of Jesus' words about divorce, it is clear that we cannot simply apply them as a casuistical legal principle in ecclesiastical ethical teaching, with which we can decide cases of morals in unbending rigidity. What is to happen when a marriage is completely shattered and ruined? May the partners separate? What, above all, should the one do who is innocent of the destruction of the marriage? May he/she try to build a new one? And what is to happen to people whose first, hastily contracted marriage has gone on the rocks but who then achieve happiness in their second marriage and lead a model family life? To these and similar questions Jesus' words give no answer. For what he wanted was in all earnestness to summon people to love and fidelity: He had no intention of creating a concrete system of matrimonial law.

Finally let us state very clearly that, by recognizing that Jesus' words on divorce are not legal principles, modern biblical scholarship does not weaken, devalue, or mitigate these words. On the contrary! They are thereby elevated (and only thus) to their full range and stature—the last radical challenge of God, which takes hold of and claims man's innermost being. Of course the Church has the right to protect marriage with her own laws, but these laws must not declare Jesus' words on divorce to be themselves a law. Before all else they must be in harmony with the entire Sermon on the Mount. As we know, there is much discussion there of mercy and forgiveness. The laws of the Church too must be merciful. Therefore it is a good sign that the Church is presently rethinking the whole question of the indissolubility of marriage and the problem of divorce; it is good that the concrete legal practice of the Church is seeking ways which on the one hand take very seriously Jesus' summons to limitless fidelity in marriage, and on the other hand give the proper place to mercy and forgiveness.

IV

HOW TO READ BIBLICAL FORMS

The third part of this book has shown that a multitude of fixed forms and genres exist in the Bible. The similitude of the poor man's lamb is in its form something different from the narrative of the revolt of Absalom; the story of Jonah is in form something different from the saga of the sacrifice of Isaac; the narrative of the arrest of Jesus is something different from the story of the Annunciation; a revelation discourse of Jesus in John's Gospel is something different from a discourse of Jesus in the Synoptics; a prophetic saying is something different from a legal statement.

We could have easily prolonged this voyage of discovery. We could have asked just what an apocalyptic discourse is, we could have concerned ourselves with the individual prophetic genres; we could have turned to the epistolary literature of the New Testament and examined its forms more closely. But then this book would have become so long that no one would read it. Moreover, it was by no means our real purpose to become acquainted in detail with all the forms and genres of the Bible. We were much more interested in acquiring a basic insight into biblical forms.

In this process it has surely become clear what importance knowledge of the structure and intent of a text has for its interpretation. Let us recall once more the words of Jesus, "Many are called, but few are chosen." A person who understands this sentence as factual information can only turn away, bewildered and depressed. But he who understands it as what it claims to be—a provocative appeal for conversion—can take it seriously and base his life upon it. Someone who reads the narrative of Jonah as a historical report will have to throw the Bible down in disgusted rage or live in intellectual schizophrenia. But, knowing that this story is a great confession of God's love for and patience with mankind, in the form of an instructive narrative, he will always read it with inner joy and constantly repeated profit.

There is, however, one more problem: What a lot of exegetical detail had to be crammed into this book in order to be able to explain structurally a very limited number of biblical texts! What about all those unexplained passages? And what of the genres and forms which could (at most) be mentioned, but not discussed? Must one not be a specialist in questions of genre if one really wishes to understand a biblical text? I don't think so.

First of all, we must not forget that in modern editions of the Bible there are a multitude of possibilities for editors and translators which can make the structure of a passage clear. If a text for example is divided into individual units (*pericopes*) and these separated by headings, it can help the reader perceive the structure more clearly, provided that the division is very careful, separating only the separable and leaving as a unit that which represents a structural unit. In the Synoptics in any case units of narrative originally handed down intact and still distinct can be relatively easily separated by paragraphs or headings. In the same way, statements of Jesus that were originally handed down in isolation and that constitute small independent units can be marked off with subheadings and indentation. Furthermore, even in a passage now coherent, older portions of tradition which were adopted by the particular author and which thus form a genre of unique kind in his text can be emphasized by typography. Thus the author of the First Letter to Timothy has incorporated into his letter an old Christological hymn. It reads:

> He was made visible in the flesh,
> attested by the Spirit,
> seen by angels,
> proclaimed to the pagans,
> believed in by the world,
> taken up in glory.
> [1 TIMOTHY 3:16]

There is probably no modern edition of the Bible in which this Christological hymn is not set off from the context by the typesetter. The case of the Logos hymn with which the author of the Fourth Gospel begins his book is similar. But the evangelist inserts a few editorial comments of his own on John the Baptist. Every good edition of Scripture here differentiates by arrangement of type between the original hymn and the interlinear comments of the evangelist.

Where aids of this sort are not applicable, the possibility still exists of indicating the genre of a biblical passage by footnotes, marginal notes, or short introductions. One must demand of a modern translation of the Bible that it not only clarify details but also give concise elucidations about questions of form and genre.

So the reader does have excellent aids, which can make many things easier and bring them closer, provided only that he really uses them. Nonetheless, all this is somewhat artificial and superficial. One best develops an instinct for recognizing biblical genres and forms just by constantly reading the Bible, especially the Old Testament. Once one has acquired a sense of literary forms such as this book has tried to provide, one is astonished when reading the Bible afterwards at the riches of genre and form there to be encountered on page after page. The more one reads, the more clearly the individual genres emerge and the more rapidly their underlying linguistic intent and application are recognized. Nothing so intensifies perception and nothing is so indispensable as frequent regular reading. The wide, immeasurable landscape of the Bible thus comes into view with ever more plasticity and color; its formations stand with increased clarity and acuity before the observer. The layman will often be unable to name the forms of representation with which he becomes familiar, but intuitively he will recognize and understand them, even without scholarly paraphernalia.

Before we now turn to the practical exercises, which we hope will broaden and deepen our form-critical knowledge, a last word is in order: We have often spoken in this book about understanding the Bible correctly. It has, I hope, become evident that it is hardly possible to understand the Bible today without at least an approximate knowledge of the forms of representation in which it speaks to us. Nonetheless, to understand the Bible well there must be something else—something which no scholarship can provide, because it reaches infinitely deeper. What I mean is best expressed by a passage from Reinhold Schneider (1903–59). It is found in his great, moving book *Veiled Day* in which he recounts his life experiences.

> One Christmas evening in Potsdam I opened the Holy Scripture. I had bought it—in Luther's translation—as a boy. After I had read a few chapters I fled into the cold dark street. For it was clear: Under this exigent claim of truth life is turned around. One cannot read this book, just as one cannot read the *Spiritual Exercises* of St. Ignatius. One can only *do* it. It's not a book at all. It is the power of life. And it is impossible to understand a single line, without the resolution to carry it out.[21]

Exercise I

The following statements provide a check for every reader to see whether he has understood this book and worked through it successfully. Over half of the 120 statements very carefully summarize the conclusions of the book. All the rest are false and contradict the text. Judge each statement as to its correctness. When in doubt, refer to the text! (The numbers of the incorrect statements are found at the end of the exercise.)

1. In all biblical narratives one must differentiate between the external form of representation and the theological statement.

2. The meaning of form criticism need be understood only by the professional exegete.

3. Variations are especially common in the opening words of letters.

4. Private letters are different in form from business letters.

5. Cooking recipes are closely related in linguistic structure to the form of directions for use.

6. The obituary notice is an established literary form.

7. Fixed forms do not exist only in written expressions of human thought; speech also frequently uses fixed and pre-established forms.

8. In the liturgy, however, there are no fixed forms.

9. Thus, for example, the classic Roman collect employs no fixed form: After all, its text is different for every Sunday.

10. Our ordinary language of daily life can run according to a fixed pattern, especially in specific, frequently recurrent conversational situations.

11. The form of a representation is always determined by its purpose.

12. Orientals greet each other in a more lively fashion and less formally than Occidentals.

13. The question "How are you?" does not necessarily intend to elicit information; it can also have the purpose of opening communication.

14. Poem, drama, short story, novella, and novel are various literary genres.

15. Every literary genre reveals reality in a different way.

16. Form criticism concerns itself with fixed forms—in everyday life or in literature, in oral and written statements; it means to discover these forms, to describe them, to determine their linguistic intent, and to determine their actual setting (*Sitz im Leben*).

17. Every new situation in which man is involved necessarily produces also new forms of speaking.

18. No fixed form is present in weather reports, because the weather situation is always changing.

19. The discovery of established forms in the Bible had been practically completed by the beginning of World War I.

20. The form of "apparition dialogue," interestingly enough, is found only in the Old Testament.

21. The joke is an established form of human speech just like the anecdote, saga, fairy tale, legend, or riddle.

22. The phrase "Once upon a time" belongs to the generic style of the fairy tale.

23. In general the Old Testament hymn begins with the so-called "conclusion."

24. Established linguistic forms are apt to follow, especially at their beginning, prescribed elements of form.

25. Prescribed structures are often employed also for the conclusion of an established form.

26. Without exception Paul's letters end with a liturgically stylized wish for blessing.

27. The revelation discourses of the Fourth Gospel end with a so-called "choral conclusion."

28. Whoever desires to describe a fixed linguistic form must not confine himself to investigation of the external structure of the form in question alone.

29. In the description of a fixed linguistic form its basic intention must also be sought.

30. Among such basic intentions are, for example, to report, to describe, to command, to forbid, to confess, to admonish, to summon, and to proclaim.

31. The Old Testament hymn is a song sung in the temple to musical accompaniment on festive occasions.

32. The "actual setting" (*Sitz im Leben*) of the hymn, accordingly, is the service of worship in the temple.

33. In contrast to the Old Testament, the New Testament has no genres whose "actual setting" is the service of worship.

34. The paradigm is a short narrative designed as an example.

35. The "actual setting" of many Old Testament proverbs was the instruction given to future officials and diplomats at the royal court.

36. Many genres of the Old Testament had their "actual setting" in social institutions.

37. The demise of these social institutions was also the end of corresponding linguistic genres.

38. The "actual setting" of a genre can never change. It is as unchangeable as the genre itself.

39. The "funeral song" represents a particular New Testament genre. It was sung at the burial of a Christian.

40. The funeral song could also be used as a song of derision.

41. The terms "form" and "genre" are used by many scholars in the same sense. Others use "form" to indicate the individual structure of a given text, whereas "genre" implies typical, frequently recurrent forms.

42. A book must always consist of a single genre; that is, it is either a novel, a collection of poetry, a scholarly treatise, or something of the sort.

43. The Bible, according to its genre, is a book of history. Its content is therefore best called "Bible history."

44. School Bibles, now out of date, used to maintain that the Bible contained an almost limitless multiplicity of the most varied forms and genres.

45. Thus the Ecker Bible distinguishes between historical narrative, saga, instructive narrative, confessional narrative, report, chronicle, similitude, parable, prophetic saying, legal saying, contract, prayer, song, revelation discourse, and revelation document.

46. It is characteristic of a similitude to narrate typical events of daily occurrence.

47. In contrast the parable narrates unusual, even unique happenings.

48. There are similitudes which can at once be recognized as similitudes by their form. But there are also similitudes which conceal themselves behind the form of a report.

49. The actual import of Jesus' similitudes is to demonstrate general religious ideas for the simple, uneducated hearer.

50. The Book of Jonah has its narrative high point in the scene in which Jonah is swallowed by the big fish.

51. The figure of Jonah is a condensation and personification of the Jewish readers whom the author is addressing.

52. The instructive character of the narrative becomes especially clear in the episode with the castor-oil plant.

53. The fish which swallows Jonah is a symbol for the great, dreadful power of paganism, which threatens believers with destruction.

54. The Book of Jonah according to its intention is neither historical writing nor biography.

55. It probably originated about the year 1400 B.C.

56. In the saga of the sacrifice of Isaac the broad description of Abraham's psychological state is especially impressive.

57. The saga of the sacrifice of Isaac must be very old; it has a long history of tradition behind it.

58. Its intent is not only to instruct but also to provide real history.

59. In a portion of the family history of Abraham it attempts to narrate a portion of the history of Israel.

60. The historical experiences deposited in the saga of the sacrifice of Isaac were extended over centuries.

61. The concept of the saga is for modern biblical scholarship not a negative but a positive concept.

62. In the form of the saga the manifold and complex experiences of an entire people could be written down in full.

63. Actual historical writing is offered in the Bible only by the New Testament.

64. The Deuteronomic history includes the five books of Moses, among which the fifth, the so-called Book of Deuteronomy, forms the conclusion and climax.

65. The principal figure of the succession history of David is Absalom, David's most famous grandson.

66. The author of this story intends Absalom as a symbol of man's revolt against God.

67. Hebron was the old residential city of David.

68. In the succession history of David it would be unthinkable that God would call down from heaven and thus intervene in history.

69. By this we can see that history is here understood from a purely secular point of view.

70. The narrative of Absalom's revolt is one of the best examples of the genre of the saga.

71. The description of Catiline's conspiracy by Sallust, in contrast to the foregoing, approaches the genre of the "treatise."

72. Telephone directories and address books belong to the genre of the list.

73. We find the genre of the list in mankind's oldest documents.

74. Lists, because of their sober enumeration of names and facts, are especially valuable for the historian.

75. The chronicle is closely related to the list.

76. The author of the Deuteronomic history incorporated into his presentation parts of royal court chronicles from Israel and Judah.

77. We do not find the genre of the official chronicle in the New Testament.

78. In Acts alone we encounter a few passages composed in the manner of a private travel journal.

79. They report the journey of Peter from Caesarea to Rome.

80. In the representation of the arrest of Jesus in Mark 14:43–52 we see, from the point of view of form, a report.

81. Later the presentation of Mark was expanded by a multiplicity of legendary themes.

82. In response to an event such as Jesus' Passion the bare documentation of externally visible facts would necessarily be inadequate.

83. The deeper meaning of such an event can be made visible only by interpretation and explanation.

84. This is the most profound reason why the genre of pure chronicle for the representation of events concerning Jesus was unsatisfactory for the primitive Church.

85. The genre of historical narrative permits incorporation of exegesis and interpretation.

86. The theme of the sixth month in Luke 1:26–38 is supposed to link the announcement of the birth of Jesus in the narrative structure with the announcement of the birth of John.

87. The structural elements of the conversation between Gabriel and Mary are largely derivative from the Old Testament.

88. The entire narrative follows two Old Testament patterns, which are combined—the pattern of proclamation and the pattern of call.

89. The center of meaning of the narrative lies in Mary's question "How can this come about?"

90. This question presupposes a vow of virginity on Mary's part.

91. Luke 1:26–38 is, according to its genre, a confessional narrative.

92. In Matthew 1–2 angels always appear in bodily form, in Luke 1–2 on the other hand always in a dream.

93. The Gospels of Luke and John are called Synoptic Gospels.

94. The linking of self-introduction and promise is often found in Jesus' discourses in John's Gospel.

95. The genre of "revelation discourse of a redeemer" is encountered not only in John's Gospel but even in the prophets of the Old Testament.

96. Typical marks of the genre of revelation discourse are self-introduction, promise, and threat.

97. The historical Jesus also often employed the genre of revelation discourse, especially in his disputation with the Pharisees.

98. The character of the preaching of Jesus cannot be fully described as prophetic.

99. Jesus, unlike the prophets, does not simply transmit a word of God which he has received, but boldly speaks as if he himself were standing in the place of God.

100. In the words of Jesus in John's Gospel the thought process begun in the Synoptics' account is carried to a finish.

101. Form criticism is the most important device in ascertaining the difference between "historical" and "not historical."

102. Jesus' words "Many are called, but few are chosen" are, according to their form, a legal saying.

103. Jesus' words on divorce are encountered in the New Testament in the most various places and at the most varied levels of tradition.

104. Jewish marriages were dissolved before a special divorce judge, who issued a so-called "writ of divorce."

105. Jewish divorce law was disadvantageous to the wife.

106. According to Jewish conception of justice, the husband could not break his own marriage at all.

107. By way of provocation, Jesus equates divorce with adultery.

108. Jesus often turns against the legal practice of the Scribes and Pharisees, but never against the Mosaic law itself.

109. As the lawgiver of the New Covenant Jesus decreed legally the indissolubility of marriage.

110. Jesus' words on divorce are composed unequivocally in the form of a legal saying.

111. Jesus' words on divorce are prophetic provocation. His intention is to uncover the deep injustice of Jewish divorce practices.

112. It is the characteristic feature of prophetic discourse to use many genres with other settings and give them a new actual setting.

113. The words on divorce in Matthew 5:32 have the same basic intention as the forbiddance of oaths, lustful looks, and anger.

114. The Bible contains a multiplicity of fixed genres and forms.

115. Knowledge of the intent of a biblical text is decisive for exegesis.

116. It should not be the function of a Bible translation to mark genres and forms for the reader.

117. There is such a thing as genuine understanding of the Bible without mastery of the scholarly technique of interpretation.

118. It is the purpose of this book to make possible in principle some insight into the genres and forms of the Bible.

119. The best insight into biblical genres and forms is obtained by frequent reading of the Bible.

120. Exercises II and III will provide additional insight.

The following statements are incorrect and contradict this book:
2, 3, 8, 9, 12, 18, 19, 20, 23, 27, 33, 37, 38, 39, 42, 43, 44, 45, 49, 50, 53, 55, 56, 63, 64, 65, 66, 69, 70, 79, 80, 89, 90, 92, 93, 95, 97, 101, 102, 104, 108, 109, 116.

Exercise II

The following exercises are supposed to provide a broader and deeper dimension to that which has already been studied. We recommend that these twenty exercises be done in writing.

1. Analyze any television quiz program as to stable elements of form—such as, for example, greeting, introduction, questioning, congratulations, sign-off. Pay special attention also to the style of the genre—that is, to phrases and formulas that are typical for quiz programs.

2. Visit a cemetery and ascertain whether there are various genres of epitaphs, or whether all of these are in fact variations on the same theme.

3. Notice how your priest or minister begins his sermon. Does he use fixed forms? Does he follow a definite pattern—for example: "Let us begin with a text from the Bible," or "Let us begin with a story"?

4. Turn the pages of the hymnal used in your church, and list all the genres in the book, such as prayer, song, litany, devotion, and so on.

5. Take any diary—your own or that of some famous person—and try to compile all the particulars of form typical of the genre "journal" or "diary."

6. Look at the Apostles' Creed. What is its basic linguistic intent?

7. Note situations of daily life in which language has a purely communicative character.

8. Determine the "actual setting" for the following genres: editorial, weather chart, creed, telegram, government document, encyclical, menu.

9. Take your daily newspaper and list the various literary genres found in a single day's issue—for example, news item, editorial, news report, advertisement, and so on.

10. Are there articles which seem to have the form of a news item, but in their linguistic intent are pure advertisement?

11. Compare the opening verses of the Epistle to the Romans, both Epistles to the Corinthians, the Epistle to the Philippians, and the Epistle to Philemon. Are there constantly recurrent elements of form? Can they be represented in a pattern?

12. Read the whole exciting history of David in 2 Samuel 9–20 and 1 Kings 1–2. As you read, look for signs of historical narrative.

13. Look up Psalm 135 in your Old Testament. Its first verse reads, "Praise the name of Yahweh!" To what genre does this psalm belong? Why? Where does the introduction end? Where does the main part begin? How does one recognize the change?

14. Examine Luke 1:46–55 as to its basic linguistic intent.

15. Matthew 7:1–14 is a composite of extremely varied sayings of Jesus, compiled at a date after he spoke them. Dissect this text into its smaller units; that is, isolate Jesus' original, independent words from one another.

16. Read Judges 13:1–7. Can you discover in this a pattern of form that you know? What is it called?

17. Look in Acts for other texts besides 21:1–10 that are composed in the form of a travel journal.

18. Look at the introduction to Luke (chapters 1 and 2) in your favorite edition of the Bible. Are certain passages set off typographically in this edition? How many? What justifies this procedure?

19. If you are intrigued by the subject of form criticism, you may want to read also Edgar V. McKnight, *What Is Form Criticism?* (Fortress Press, Phila., 1969). Other works on the subject are listed in its bibliography.

20. Determine the genre and the basic linguistic intent of the twenty exercises just completed.

Exercise III

We come now to the most important and difficult part of our exercises. Here are twenty passages from the Old and New Testaments. Some of them consist only of single sentences. Try to determine the genre and the linguistic intent of each, and in addition find out what book of the Bible is the source. For example:

> "Our Father in heaven,
>   may your name be held holy,
>   your kingdom come. . . ."

Genre: prayer   Intention: petition   Source: Matthew

In order to facilitate your work, we list the genres to which the quoted texts belong, though not, of course, in the same order: foretelling the future, similitude with dative beginning, proverb, list, report of a vision, letter, love song, similitude with nominative beginning, curse, hymn, funeral song, prophetic saying, prayer, revelation discourse, legal saying, admonition, travel journal, preaching, chronicle, beatitude.

1. "I am the bread of life.
   He who comes to me will never be hungry;
   he who believes in me will never thirst. . . ."

2. Sailing from Troas we made a straight run for Samothrace; the next day for Neapolis, and from there for Philippi, a Roman colony and the principal city of that particular district of Macedonia. . . .

3. The man who commits adultery with his neighbor's wife must die, he and his accomplice.

4. "I tell you solemnly, this day, this very night, before the cock crows twice, you will have disowned me three times."

5. Better a poor man healthy and fit than a rich man tormented in body.

6. In the fourth year of Hezekiah, which was the seventh year of Hoshea son of Elah, king of Israel, Shalmaneser king of Assyria made war on Samaria and laid seige to it. He captured it after three years.

7. Come, let us praise Yahweh joyfully,
   acclaiming the Rock of our safety;
   let us come into his presence with thanksgiving,
   acclaiming him with music.
   For Yahweh is a great God,
   a greater King than all other gods. . . .

8. "You blind guides! Straining out gnats and swallowing camels!"

9. Jacob's sons numbered twelve. The sons of Leah: Jacob's eldest son Reuben, then Simeon, Levi, Judah, Issachar and Zebulun. The sons of Rachel: Joseph and Benjamin. The sons of Bilhah, Rachel's slave-girl: Dan and Naphtali. The sons of Zilpah, Leah's slave-girl: Gad and Asher. These are the sons born to Jacob in Paddan-aram.

10. Now as he was speaking, a woman in the crowd raised her voice and said, "Happy the womb that bore you, and the breasts you sucked!"

11. "You shall crawl on your belly and eat dust every day of your life."

12. "This is what the kingdom of God is like. A man throws seed on the land. Night and day, while he sleeps, when he is awake, the seed is sprouting and growing; how, he does not know."

13. Oh, how lonely she sits,
    the city once thronged with people,
    as if suddenly widowed.
    Though once great among the nations,
    she, the princess among provinces,
    is now reduced to vassalage.
    She passes her nights weeping;

the tears run down her cheeks.
Not one of all her lovers remains to comfort her.
Her friends have all betrayed her
and become her enemies.

14. "There was a judge in a certain town who had neither fear of God nor respect for man."

15. "Abba (Father)! Everything is possible for you. Take this cup away from me. But let it be as you, not I, would have it."

16. Be happy at all times; pray constantly; and for all things give thanks to God, because this is what God expects you to do in Christ Jesus. Never try to suppress the Spirit or treat the gift of prophecy with contempt; think before you do anything—hold on to what is good and avoid every form of evil.

17. "Claudius Lysias to his Excellency the governor Felix, greetings. This man had been seized by the Jews and would have been murdered by them but I came on the scene with my troops and got him away, having discovered that he was a Roman citizen."

18. My Beloved lifts up his voice,
he says to me,
"Come then my love,
my lovely one, come.
For see, winter is past,
The rains are over and gone.
The flowers appear on the earth.
The season of glad songs has come,
the cooing of the turtledove is heard
in our land.
The fig tree is forming its first figs
and the blossoming vines give out their fragrance."

19. Christ died for our sins in accordance with the Scriptures; . . . he was buried, he was raised to life on the third day, in accordance with the scrpitures; . . . he appeared first to Cephas and secondly to the Twelve.

20. Then I saw a great white throne and the One who was sitting on it. In his presence earth and sky vanished, leaving no trace. I saw the dead, both great and small, standing in front of his throne, while the book of life was opened, and other books opened which were the record of what they had done in their lives, by which the dead were judged.

KEY TO EXERCISE III

1. Revelation discourse, revealing, John 6:35.

2. Travel journal, reporting, Acts 16:11–12.

3. Legal saying, decreeing, Leviticus 20:10.

4. Foretelling the future, prediction, Mark 14:30.

5. Proverb, instruction, Ecclesiasticus 30:14.

6. Chronicle, reporting, 2 Kings 18:9–10.

7. Hymn, praising, Psalm 95 (94):1–3.

8. Prophetic saying, provocation, Matthew 23:24.

9. List, enumeration, Genesis 35:23–26.

10. Beatitude, praise, Luke 11:27.

11. Curse, cursing, Genesis 3:14.

12. Similitude with dative beginning, instruction, Mark 4:26–27.

13. Funeral song, lament, Lamentations 1:1–2.

14. Similitude with nominative beginning, Luke 18:2.

15. Prayer, petition, Mark 14:36.

16. Admonition, admonishing, 1 Thessalonians 5:16–22.

17. Letter, communication, Acts 23:26–27.

18. Love song, wooing, Song of Songs 2:10–13.

19. Preaching, proclamation, 1 Corinthians 15:3–5.

20. Report of a vision, communication, Revelation 20:11–12.

NOTES

1. K. Tucholsky, *Zwischen Gestern und Morgen. Eine Auswahl aus seinen Schriften und Gedichten* (Hamburg, 1952), 8.

2. Cf. W. Thesiger, *Arabian Sands* (New York, Dutton, 1959), 87–88.

3. A. Jolles, *Einfache Formen* (Tübingen, 1930).

4. R. Lettau, *Auftritt Manigs*, in *prosa viva* 1 (Munich: Carl Hanser Verlag, 1963).

5. For details cf. G. Lohfink, *The Conversion of St. Paul* (Chicago: Franciscan Herald Press, 1976).

6. Cf. for example O. Eissfeldt, *The Old Testament: An Introduction* (New York: Harper & Row, 1965).

7. M. Dibelius, *From Tradition to Gospel* (New York: Scribner's, 1965).

8. Quoted in A. Holl, *Jesus in schlechter Gesellschaft* (Stuttgart, 1971), 173.

9. J. W. von Goethe, *Die Leiden des jungen Werther* (*The Sorrows of Young Werther*) trans. R. D. Boylan, ed. Victor Lange (New York: Rinehart, 1956), 104–5.

10. J. Ecker, *Katholische Schulbibel für die Diözese Limburg* (Düsseldorf: 1929), 309.

11. J. Jeremias, *The Parables of Jesus*, trans. S. H. Hook (New York: Scribner's, 1963).

12. Cf. the great analysis of H. W. Wolff, *Studien zum Jonabuch* (*Biblische Studien* 47) (Neukirchen-Vluyn, 1965), esp. 53.

13. Cf. Wolff, op. cit., 48–49, 77–83.

14. G. von Rad, *Genesis: A Commentary*, trans. John H. Marks, (Philadelphia, Westminster Press, 1961).

15. Formulated with support from G. von Rad, *Old Testament Theology* (New York: Harper & Row, 1962).

16. Translation by Daniel Coogan.

17. The text of Celsus is given by Origen, *Contra Celsum*, VII, 9.

18. M. Lidzbarski, *Das Johannesbuch der Mandäer* (Giessen, 1915), 154–56.

19. M. Lidzbarski, *Ginza: Der Schatz oder Das grosse Buch der Mandäer* (Göttingen, 1925), 58–60.

20. Cf. E. Fuchs, *Studies of the Historical Jesus* (London: Allenson, 1964).

21. R. Schneider, *Verhüllter Tag* (Herder-Bücherei 42) Freiburg, 1961, 108.